Rich'Diakula

Study Guide and Workbook
Michael Vengrin

ABOUT PHILOSOPHY

FOURTH EDITION

Robert Paul Wolff
University of Massachusetts

 PRENTICE HALL, *Englewood Cliffs, New Jersey 07632*

D1416207

Editorial/production supervision and
 interior design: *Dominic J. Pandiscia*
Manufacturing buyer: *Peter Havens*

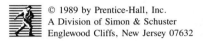 © 1989 by Prentice-Hall, Inc.
A Division of Simon & Schuster
Englewood Cliffs, New Jersey 07632

Printed in the United States of America

10 9 8 7 6 5 4 3 2 1

ISBN   0-13-000456-1

Prentice-Hall International (UK) Limited, *London*
Prentice-Hall of Australia Pty. Limited, *Sydney*
Prentice-Hall Canada Inc., *Toronto*
Prentice-Hall Hispanoamericana, S.A., *Mexico*
Prentice-Hall of India Private Limited, *New Delhi*
Prentice-Hall of Japan, Inc., *Tokyo*
Simon & Schuster Asia Pte. Ltd., *Singapore*
Editora Prentice-Hall do Brasil, Ltda., *Rio de Janeiro*

CONTENTS

PREFACE

As you will soon discover, philosophy is not the easiest of
subjects to study, nor is it the easiest to teach!
However, for those of us who are engaged in the teaching or
doing of philosophy, it is a most important and valuable
area. I hope that one of the consequences of your taking a
philosophy course is your coming to appreciate its
signficance for your own life and the impact that it has
had on people in the past.

The purpose of this Study Guide is to help you get the most
out of the textbook. You should view it as a **supplement** to
your text and certainly not as something to read in place
of it.

I want to comment on some of the features of this Study
Guide, but first a few suggestions for using it in
conjunction with your textbook. I would recommend that
before you read a certain chapter in the Wolff text, that
you first read the Chapter Overview which is provided in
this study guide. When you read a chapter for the first
time, you do not usually know what it is about, although
the chapter heading may give you some clue. The chapter
overview is intended to give you a kind of perspective for
the chapter that should make it easier to read and
understand. It's kind of like having a road map of an
unfamiliar area; after looking at the map, you have some
idea of the territory and its landmarks. For some of you
who like to pursue uncharted areas, this approach may not
be as exciting.

Secondly, I would encourage you to reread the chapters. I
tell my own students to do this, but I suspect that they
only heed this advice the night before the test. Of
course, this is not what I mean when I say to reread the
chapter. The idea is that the first reading will provide
you with the main point, question, or issue that is
examined. The second reading will be more analytic in
nature; you will seek an understanding of the problems and
issues, look for answers, and attempt the appraise them.
You may think that I have taken leave of my senses, but I
am in earnest in what I say; and I believe you will be
amply rewarded for your efforts. I know that reading such
a thing as a philosophy textbook is hard work (some of my
students use other words to describe it), but I would like
to encourage you to develop study techniques, such as a second

reading, which really will result in you getting the most out of your study, with the least input. At least give it one try.
Another feature of the Study Guide is the inclusion of Study Suggestions for each chapter. These contain information on which terms you need to know in order to understand the main ideas of the chapter. Quite frequently, the study suggestions will warn you of a section of the chapter that you may have difficulty with. Given the nature of the information contained in this section, I would recommend that you also read it prior to reading the chapter or at least prior to the second reading.

For each chapter of the Wolff text, there is an analysis of each section; the section division numbers correspond to those of the textbook. Sometimes, the analysis is a synopsis of the particular section; at other times, it is an explanation of major ideas that Wolff has presented. I have tried to focus on the fundamental issues that are being examined in the main text. Please, read this section of the Study Guide **after** you have read the textbook material. It is here, that I feel that some of you may attempt to use the Study Guide as a substitute for the textbook. There is much more in the textbook than what has been covered in this section of the Study Guide, so do not deny yourself the opportunity of learning that material.

A Chapter Outline follows the Chapter Analysis section. The main (perhaps, only) value of a chapter outline is that it gives you the underlying structure of the chapter. Probably, the best time to read it is after the first reading.

A list of Key Terms comes after the Chapter Analysis section. Important terms that are used in the textbook chapters are briefly defined. The terms that are preceded with an asterisk (*) are also defined in the Wolff text, usually in a more complete manner. You will notice that many ordinary words are used in philosophy with a much different meaning, so do pay close attention to terminology. And one last note on definitions: you may find your course instructor providing you with a definition that differs from the ones in this Study Guide or the textbook. Philosophic terms are defined differently by different philosophers.

I think that one of the most useful sections of the Study Guide is the "Check List of Important Items." It is a listing of important terms, thinkers, and writings. A knowledge of the terms listed here is essential to an understanding of the problems and issues that Wolff examines in the textbook. I would recommend that after you have studied a particular chapter, that you go to the list of terms and see if you can give an explanation of each item in the list. This is really a self test. I suggest to my own students, that they make up flash cards (3x5 index cards) with one term on the front and a definition or explanation of the term on the back. Use the cards (which are mixed up; some have definitions face up, others the term face up. Also the order of the cards should be random.) as a self test. If you find yourself drawing a mental blank as you read one of the terms on the front of the card, this should tell you something -you do not know the term well enough. Turn the card over and study it. Make up cards for the various thinkers and the writings.

Your best guide for what you need to know about the thinkers and writings is the professor of your course. There is a great deal of variation here, but you will probably have to know which thinkers are associated with which of the various theories, problems, and issues.

The last section in each chapter of the Study Guide contains two self tests. The first is an objective type test, and the second uses the essay format. Answers are provided to all of the questions in the objective tests; these appear in the Appendix at the end of the Study Guide.

I hope you find that this supplement to your text makes the study of philosophy a little easier.

Chapter One

What is Philosophy?

Study Suggestions

As you read through this chapter, keep in mind the question
that Wolff uses as part of the title of the first three
sections - what do philosophers do? Look for specific
answers in the three sections and relate these to
particular thinkers. Also, you should begin to form an
idea of what counts as a philosophical question. Doing
this will develop some insights into the nature of
philosophy. Be careful as you study sections four and
five, since the focus changes somewhat from the first three
sections. The discussion of the nature of the universe and
human nature shifts to a discussion of the nature of
philosophy in section four and the usefulness of philosophy
in section five.

Chapter Overview

This chapter is a general introduction to the discipline of
philosophy and focuses on the question of what philosophers
do. One of the things that philosophers do is to ask and
answer certain kinds of questions. It presents human
nature and the nature of the universe as two basic areas of
concern that philosophers ask questions about. Socrates
and the Milesians are discussed as philosophers who have
made major contributions in these respective areas. But
other philosophers are interested in both areas and seek to
understand the relation between. The philosophical
theories of the Stoics and David Hume are discussed in this
context. Lastly there are philosophers and others who

raise questions concerning the nature of philosophy itself
and what it is that philosophers should be doing.
Wittgenstein and Plato serve as representatives of this
approach.

Chapter Analysis

Section I

As you read through this section, look carefully for
answers to the question of what philosophers do. Section I
deals with Socrates as an example of a philosopher whose
primary concern was human nature. After a brief account of
his life and three events which lead to his fame, there is
a discussion of four basic principles which he used in the
examination of life. These four principles are summarized
below.

1. The unexamined life is not worth living.
2. There are valid, objective principles of thought
   and action which must be followed in order to
   lead a good life.
3. True principles of thought and action reside
   within each individual.
4. Certain individuals- men like Socrates- can aid
   men in self-examination so that they become aware
   of these principles.

As Socrates traveled about the various meeting places in
Athens and attempted to institute some of the principles,
he encountered many individuals with minds closed to the
illumination of any truth. One of the methods which he
developed to gain entry to such individuals was the use of
irony. Professor Wolff explains irony as a kind of verbal
judo - a form of communication - which has the following
elements:
1. A double audience- the superficial and the real
   audience.
2. The speaker uses statements which have a double
   meaning.
3. The superficial audience understands only the
   superficial meaning of the statments, while the
   real audience understands both the superficial
   and the intended meanings.
The irony is that the first audience is in a state of
ignorance concerning the intended or real meaning of the
speaker, although they do not realize it; the second
audience is aware of the ignorance of the first as well as
the real meaning of the speaker. Socrates' use of irony
often involved the profession of ignorance as a way of
beginning a dialogue with an opponent. The point of

Socratic irony was to lead the person into an awareness of their own ignorance so that they might then begin to pursue the truth.

Along with irony Socrates also used the dialectical method as a way of discovering truth. The method is a process of one person putting forth a thesis which is then analyzed by the other participants -usually Socrates in Plato's dialogues. The analysis of the thesis will normally reveal certain inconsistencies or contradictions. The thesis is revised so as to remove these, and the process continues. The goal is to arrive at some refined thesis that all the participants accept as true; however, this rarely happens in Plato's dialogues. Read Socrates' debate with Thrasymachus at the end of the first section and look to see how Socrates uses this method.

Section II

This section provides you with another answer to the question of what philosophers do and that is that they ask questions about the ultimate nature of reality. Of course, they also provide answers to their questions as you have already discovered in your reading of this section. The question raised by the Milesians -Thales, Anaximander, and Anaximenes- comes to this: is there some single element out of which everything is composed? This question may not strike you as philosophical but rather as scientific. And this would be a correct way to think of it, but science at this time -about 600 B.C.- was not a separate discipline.

The importance of this question is that it represents an attempt to understand the world and the universe. Earlier and some later civilizations took the universe for granted, but these Greek thinkers wanted to know why things were as they were. In essence, this was the beginning of philosophy and also of science.

By now you may be beginning to realize that one of the major characteristics of philosophy and philosophers is the asking of questions. But now consider some of their answers which Wolff discusses. For Thales, ultimate reality is water and for Anaximenes it is air. These answers may seem overly simplistic but this, remember, was only the beginning of the process of man attempting to gain an understanding of his universe. Latter thinkers would refine these answers. One important point to note in this section is some of the common assumptions of the Milesians. Indeed, the questions they asked and the answers they gave clearly indicate that they regarded

ultimate reality in terms of **one** basic element. The second
assumption was that man could understand the universe in
naturalistic terms without bringing in his religious
beliefs. The Lucretius reading presents another answer
-atoms- to the same question raised by Thales and also
illustrates the two assumptions listed above.

The last two selections from Science News on modern
cosmologies reveal another important characteristic of
philosophical questions - they are timeless. As these
selections show, the search started by Thales continues,
and as you read later chapters from your philosophy
textbook, you will find that many questions asked by
philosophers of the past are still being addressed by
twentieth century thinkers.

Section III

Section III is an examination of the attempt by
philosophers to discover the relation between the universe
and man. You might understand it as an attempt to
understand man and his place in the whole scheme of things.

Wolff presents two strategies that were used by thinkers to
bring a kind of synthesis of the study of the universe and
the study of human nature. Below is a summary of the
first.

> Strategy I: This involves the concept of natural
> law -the idea that the entire universe
> behaves in an orderly manner. Thus,
> all thing in the universe, including
> man, reflect this order. Since the
> universe and human nature have this
> underlying unity, the study of this
> order would lead to an understanding of
> both.

At the beginning of Section III, the Stoics are introduced
as one group of thinkers who used this strategy . They
used the term logos instead of the term, natural law, for
the underlying order that permeates the universe and man
himself. The reading from Marcus Aurelius is used to
illustrate the Stoic approach.

The second strategy, which was used by philosophers of the
seventeenth and eighteenth centuries, is outlined below.

> Strategy II: This approach uses epistemology -the
> study of knowledge- as the basis for
> understanding nature. The idea is that
> if one understands the knowing process
> for man, that is, how man comes to have

the knowledge he has, then one can also
obtain some understanding of the
universe at the same time.
Wolff has chosen David Hume as representative of this
second stragegy and has listed three points contained in
the selected reading from Hume. As you read the passage,
you should attempt to find these and to understand them in
the context of strategy II. The three points can be
sumarized as follows:
1. The different sciences and other fields of study
    can be turned into a unified study of human
    nature.
2. It is necessary to study ideas since they are
    employed in the statements that are made in the
    sciences, religion and politics.
3. It is necessary to study the reasoning process.

Section IV

This section may strike you as strange, to say the
least. Indeed, you may be pondering why philosophers would
attack philosophy- the very thing they do. What this
section reveals is that there are no bounds to
philosophical questioning. Philosophers do ask questions
about what philosophy should be.

In this section, Wittgenstein is introduced as a
philosopher who raised the issue of the nature of
philosophical problems. His own position was that there
were no genuine philosophical problems at all, but rather
confusion in the writing and thinking of philosophers
themselves. The task of philosophy was not the solving of
problems but the dissolving of problems; that is, showing
the person that the so called problem was only the result
of some kind of confusion. Once the confusion is
eliminated, there is no problem to be solved. For
Wittgenstein then, philosophy in not the study of the
nature of reality, nor is it the study of human nature, but
a kind of therapy to be practiced by those who think there
really are philosophical problems.

Section V

The last section of the chapter is, first, a brief summary
of five different concepts of what philosophy is. These
have all been discussed in the previous sections. Secondly,
this section presents a criticism of philosophy by no less
than one of the most important Western philosphers, Plato!
The selection from Plato might be viewed as raising a

question concerning the usefulness of philosophy. To be sure, you will probably find yourself asking the same thing as you study philosophy. You should not conclude, of course, that Plato thought that the study of philosophy was useless simply because he raised the issue.

Chapter One Outline

Section One: What Do Philosophers Do? The Study of Human
               Nature

   I.   Socrates as an example.

  II.   The elements which lead to Socrates fame.

        A.   Plato's dialogues.
        B.   The trial and death of Socrates.
        C.   The Socratic Method.

 III. Four Socratic principles.

        A.   The examination of life.
        B.   The existence of objective principles of
               thought and action.
        C.   The existence of inner truth.
        D.   The role of teachers and others.

  IV.   Socratic irony.

   V.   The Thrasymachus-Socrates debate.

Section Two: What Do Philosophers Do? The Study of the
               Universe

   I.   The cosmology of the Milesians.

        A.   The basic substance of reality.
        B.   Naturalistic explanations.

  II.   The atomism of Lucretius.

 III. Philosophy and modern cosmology.

Section Three: What Do Philosophers Do? Human Nature and
               the Universe

   I.   The Stoic strategy.

        A.   The idea of order.
        B.   The idea of natural law.
        C.   Marcus Aurelius as an example.

  II.   The modern strategy.

      A.   The study of knowledge.

      B.   David Hume's theory.

Section Four: Philosophers Attack Philosophy

     I.   Philosophical problems.

    II. Wittgenstein's approach.

Section Five:

     I.   The different conceptions of philosophy.

    II. Plato's criticism of philosophy.

KEY TERMS

*Philosophy	The word comes from a Greek word which means love of wisdom. The word seems to have been first used by Pythagoras, an early Greek thinker who lived about 572-497 B.C.
Dialogue	A literary style of writing involving two of more speakers who are engaged in a kind of question and answer discussion. Plato uses this form of writing with Socrates as the major speaker.
*Dialectical Method	A method, used by Socrates, of asking questions and critically analyzing answers as a way to arrive at propositions that can be accepted as true. Sometimes this is referred to as the Socratic Method.
Irony	A literary method used by Socrates as a way of engaging people in debate or discussion. The use of irony requires two audiences and a double meaning to the speakers statements. The first or superficial audience only understands the surface meaning of the statement; whereas the second or real audience understands both the superficial and the real meaning of the statement.
*Cosmology	The study and explanation of the universe. The pre-socratics -philosophers who lived prior to Socrates- were among the first thinkers to embark on such a study.
Milesians	A term used to refer to the first three philosophers- Thales, Anaximander, and Anaximenes.
Atomism	The cosmological theory which states that all objects are composed in invisible entities

called atoms. Lucretius was a
defender of this view.

*Epistemology   The branch of philosophy that
                       studies the nature, sources, and
                       extent of human knowledge. The
                       word also is used to refer to a
                       person's theory of knowledge.

*Rationalism   The theory of knowledge which
                       states that the ultimate source of
                       knowledge is reason.

*Empiricism   The theory of knowledge which
                       states that the ultimate source of
                       knowledge is the senses.

Check List of Important Items

TERMS

Philosophy   Cosmology   Natural law
Dialogue   Milesians   Logos
Irony   Stoics   Epistemology
Dialectical method   Empiricism   Rationalism

THINKERS

Socrates   Plato   Thales
Ananimander   Anaximenes   Lucretius
Marcus Aurelius   David Hume   Immanuel Kant
Ludwig Wittgenstein

WRITINGS

Republic   On The Nature of Things

A Treatise of Human Nature   Philosophical Investigations

A Critique of Pure Reason   Gorgias

SELF TEST I

1.   Which of the following would best represent the
     position of Socrates concerning knowledge? 1. its
     acquisition requires the method of irony 2. it lies

10

within the individual but may be accessed by
self-examination 3. it can only be achieved with the
aid of teachers 4. it is subjective or relative to
the individual.

2. According to the Stoics the universe is governed by
which of the following? 1. fate 2. logos or order
3. cause and effect 4. they do not view the universe
as having order.

3. The individual given credit as being the Western
world's first philosopher is: 1. Socrates 2.
Plato 3. Thales 4. Pythagoras.

4. This thinker was presented as an atomist.
_____.

5. The two basic concerns of early philosophers were the
nature of the universe and the nature of man. In
which was Socrates most interested?

6. Which of the following best represents the position of
Wittgenstein on the nature of philosophy? 1. he
believes that philosophy should explain the nature of
the universe 2. he maintains that philosophy is a
kind of conceptual confusion 3. he states that
self-examination is the best approach to philosophical
problems 4. he claims that the study of human nature
is the very core of philosophy.

7. This philosopher was presented in the text to
illustrate the strategy of studying nature by studying
the knowing process in man. 1. Marcus Aurelius 2.
Plato 3. Wittgenstein 4. David Hume.

8. The study of the nature, sources and extent of human
knowledge is called _____.

9. One of the methods used by Socrates was irony. Which
of the following best represents his use of it? 1. he
employed it to ridicule his opponents 2. he used it
to try to convince his opponents that they did not
know as much as they were claiming to know 3. he used
it as a means of entertaining his disciples 4. he
used irony a method for the examination of literature.

10. Wolff maintains that cosmological speculation ended
with Socrates, that later thinkers focused primarily
on human nature to the neglect of this area. True
False.

11. This dialogue of Plato is presented as containing a criticism of philosophy. _____

12. The cosmological theories of the Milesians have some common assumptions about the nature of reality. Which of the following is one of these? 1. there is one basic substance or element 2. reality can only be explained on the basis of a belief in God or gods 3. everything is composed of a combination of water, earth, air, and fire; no single one of these is a basic element 4. ultimate reality is continually changing.

13. Of all of the philosophers presented in this chapter, which one was discussed as the most famous? _____

14. According to Wolff, the early Greek philosophers could also be refered to as scientists. True False.

15. There are three events which are discussed as leading to Socrates' reputation and fame. Plato's dialogues and the trial of Socrates are two of these. What is the other?

SELF TEST II

1. List and give a short explanation of the four principles that were basic to Socrates' philosophy.

2. Give a short description of irony and how Socrates would use it.

3. Briefly explain the term cosmology and its relation to the Milesians.

4. Wolff suggests two separate strategies that were used by the Stoics and then by modern philosophers like David Hume to unify the study of reality with that of human nature. Explain these strategies.

5. How is Wittgenstein's approach to philosophy different from that of Socrates?

6. What are some of the criticisms of philosophy that have been raised in this chapter? Do you think that they are justified?

7. Explain the dialectical method and its use by Socrates.

8. Three sections of this chapter have been concerned with the issue of what philosophers do. You have found, most certainly, that one of the things they do is to ask questions. List what you think would be some representative philosophical questions.

9. For each of the following philosophers, list a few major ideas that would be associated with each one:
   1. Socrates
   2. David Hume
   3. Marcus Aurelius
   4. Wittgenstein
   5. Lucretius

10. Notice the title of this first chapter - What is Philosophy? After having read this chapter , how would you now answer this question?

Chapter Two

Ethics

Study Suggestions

As you read through section II, try to get an understanding
of the three reasons for studying ethics that Wolff
discusses. Then, as you read sections III and IV and V,
see how each reason is examined there in relation to a
major thinker. Make associations between the thinkers that
are presented and the particular reason for studying ethics
that is being discussed. Also, clue in on some of the
problems and objections which Wolff raises to the answers
which the thinkers present. Finally, as you read the
section on Contemporary Application, look for the
application of such things as Kant's categorical imperative
and Bentham's principle of utilitarianism.

Chapter Overview

Ethics is the branch of philosophy which, to put it simply,
studies morality, and this chapter is an introduction to
this area. The three main questions which are examined
are:
1. Are there any universally sound moral principles;
   if so, how are they validated?
2. How do we solve moral dilemmas, cases in which
   there is genuine doubt about what is right and
   what is wrong?
3. What is the "good life?"
The moral philosophy of Immanuel Kant is presented as one
answer to the first question. The utilitarianism of Jeremy

Bentham is discussed for the second and Plato's answer is examined for the last.

Chapter Analysis

Section I

Section I contains biographical material on Immanuel Kant, so you will have some understanding of the circumstances in which he developed his moral philosophy. Also, Wolff presents two main problems that were of concern to Kant. The first problem was that of reconciling the idea that human beings have free will with the assumption that was used in science, that the events of the universe are caused. The second problem was that of providing some kind of proof for fundamental moral principles. Later, in Section III, you will find how Kant deals with this latter problem. The first problem is not really discussed any further.

Section II

The structure of the rest of the chapter is outlined in section II. Here Wolff raises three reasons to think about ethics. He also refers to these as "three searches." Below is a list of the three:
1. The search for "absolutely certain, universally valid first principles of conduct " that can be, in some sense, proven.
2. "The search for a method or process of reasoning to help us in deciding hard cases."
3. "The search for the good life."
You will find a detailed examination of each of these, respectively, in the next three sections.

Section III

The first several paragraphs of section III may not seem to you to be dealing with the first of the above listed searches. What Wolff is doing here is developing a background against which Kant may be introduced. The issue these paragraphs introduce is that of the differences in morals, individually and culturally; what one individual or culture approves another condemns. There are three approaches discussed as to how the issue can be handled. A summary of the three follows.
1. The denial that there are any variations.

2. The admission of variations with the implication that there are no absolute or objective moral principles.
3. The admission of the variations with the claim that there are at least some objective moral principles.

Wolff briefly discusses the denial of variations of morals and lists David Hume as one who took this approach. Despite the evidence from anthropology, the argument is that there is only a surface disagreement. The "variations" constitute a factual disagreement which mask an underlying agreement about objective principles. The example of the Christian Scientist and the one of abortion are used to illustrate this point.

In examining the second approach, Wolff presents two different forms of the denial of objective moral principles. These are:
1. ethical skepticism - the claim that there can be no certainty about moral principles.
2. ethical relativism - the claim that all moral principles are relative to the individual or group.

As you read the passage from Ruth Benedict, you might try to state what you think her argument is in support of ethical relativism.

The remainder of section III is an examination of Kant's moral system as a rebuttal of both the ethical skeptic and the ethical relativist. As you study this part of the chapter, first, get a general understanding of Kant's system and then, see how he has provided a kind of refutation of both skepticism and relativism. Wolff explains Kants moral system as containing three fundamental elements and these must be understood in order to comprehend Kant's system. These three elements are summarized below.
1. Individuals are rational beings; that is, persons have the ability to make choices on the basis of reason and to act on the choices.
2. Individuals have an intrinsic value; that is people have value in and of themselves.
3. Individuals are the authors of moral law.

These elements are really bound up in Kant's moral principle which he calls the categorical imperative -"Act only on that maxim through which you can at the same time will that it should be come universal law." You will, probably, find the statement of this principle to be somewhat awkward the first time you read it, so re-read it a couple more times, and try to get some insight into what Kant is saying. The examples that Wolff presents should be of help. The point of the categorical imperative is to determine whether or not an action is one that one ought to do. Notice, though, that the conclusion that one person reaches -about whether to do the act or not- should be the same for all who apply the imperative. Kant argues that it will be the same, if the three above listed elements are all satisfied. Thus, there would be morals that are both objective and valid.

Another point to keep in mind concerning the categorical imperative is that it is a self-imposed moral principle that is the product of one's own reason and nature. This is the upshot to the text discussion of the term "autonomos" and, also, one of the points raised in the last reading from Kant. So there is no misunderstanding of Kant's moral principle, let me remind you of one important thing that Professor Wolff stated about Kant back in section I. There he stated that the main moral issue for Kant was not one of answering the question, "What should I do?" For Kant, most people already know what is right and wrong. The use of his imperative, then, is not so much one of helping us to decide what ought to be done as it is that of justifying that it is the right thing to be done or not done.

Section IV

This section is an introduction to the moral system of Jeremy Bentham which is called utilitariansim. This system is presented as an examination of the second reason for studying ethics (refer to section II above for the list of these). The basic principle of utilitarianism is stated in the beginning of the second paragraph of this section and is the heart of Bentham's system. Here is one version of the principle: seek the greatest good for the greatest number. It is important to note that Bentham uses the terms "good," "happiness," and "pleasure" as synonymous. He is proposing, what some philosophers have called, a social hedonism. Hedonism, you may know, is a moral theory which advocates the seeking of pleasure and the avoidance of pain, in so far as this is possible.

Wolff presents Bentham's philosophy as one which could be used to answer the "hard questions" of morality concerning what one ought to do. The proposal, so far, is this: one ought to do that which produces the greatest good -pleasure- for the greatest number. How does one know

whether an act has this character? In answer, Bentham has
provided a hedonic calculus. In theory, one could add up
all the consequences of an act and assign to them so many
units of pleasure or pain. The goal is to secure a balance
of pleasure over pain, so, a simple calculation would
reveal what one ought to do. See Wolff's illustration of
the young man who is trying to decide whether or not he
should leave home. This is an application of Bentham's
method.

You should keep in mind that Wolff is only giving you an
outline of Bentham's system and that there are a great many
details that have been left out. Nevertheless, you should
have a good idea of what is involved in using the principle
of utilitarianism in making a moral decision.

Three strengths of Bentham's proposal are discussed next;
their summary follows.
>   1.   The theory of utilitarianism is simplistic in
>   that it uses terms, like pleasure, that all
>   people understand.
>   2.   The theory does not require "strange, painful
>   sacrifices from its believers."
>   3.   The system is easy to apply; that is, one knows
>   what to do, how to calculate, in making a
>   decision.

The reading from Bentham which follows these will give you
some insights about how he thought the principle of
utilitarianism could be used to bring about social reforms.
Indeed, in the next chapter, you will find utilitarianism
presented as a social theory!

The last part of section IV deals with a kind of appraisal
of utilitarianism. Despite the strengths which were
outlined above, Wolff suggests some serious objections, to
this moral theory. The two criticisms which are examined
are these:
>   1.   It is not clear what is meant by "maximizing"
>   happiness.
>   2.   It -utilitarianism- can be used to justify
>   actions that most people would claim to be
>   wrong.

Wolff shows how the term maximum happiness could be
reasonably rendered as the "greatest average happiness" so
that most of the sting is removed from the first objection.
The second objection, however, seems to be difficult or
impossible to refute so it represents a serious flaw in
Bentham's system.

Section V.

The last of the three reasons for studying ethics concerns the search for the "good life" and this is the topic of Section V. It may seem to you that this section has little to do with ethics as you have come to understand it, and that this is another one of those bewildering areas of philosophy; but, perhaps, this is due to our contemporary conception of morality which tends to focus on the rightness or wrongness of particular acts. However, to the early Greek thinkers like Socrates, Plato, Aristotle, and others, ethics is concerned with the whole of one's life. It did not focus merely on specific acts or actions but rather on the sum total of them.

To understand this section then, you must grasp their conception of ethics as dealing with the whole of life. It is important to note that these thinkers used terms like "just" and "unjust" rather than "moral" or "immoral" in their discussions of ethics. For them, the leading of a just life was equivalent to living the good life. To discover the nature of justice was to discover the nature of the good life. So, as you study this section, keep in mind that their approach to morality is somewhat different than our own.

In the second paragraph of this section, Wolff introduces the major topic which will be examined in the rest of the chapter. The issue is "the proper internal order of the self." The nature of this internal order is explained and illustrated, first, with reference to Plato, and then to Erikson.
In the Republic, Plato defines individual justice as a balance or harmony of three elements of the soul or the self which are these:
1. The rational element, reason.
2. The spirited element, the tendency to act brave or cowardly.
3. The desires, our various drives for food, drink, etc.
The just person is one in which this harmony exists. Note from the text discussion of Plato's theory, that this balance is brought about by the person, it does not merely happen. For example, the individual must assert his rational control over the spirited element or the desires. Moreover, the individual who brings about this balance throughout his life is living the good life, and for Plato, is acting morally. As you read the selection from the Republic, be sure to take note of the nature of injustice.

The nature of inner harmony for Erikson, Wolff suggests, is "very much like what Plato called wisdom," and the term

used to describe it is "ego integrity." One major
difference between the theory of Plato and that of Erikson
is that for Plato the harmony of the self can be brought
about immediately, but notice, because of how ego integrity
is defined, it can only be achieved in old age. Erikson
does not mean that those who die young have
not lived the good life, since they could have resolved
various crises successfully at each stage. It's just that
they have been denied the opportunity to complete the whole
cycle. But even for Plato, a certain amount of time is
required to achieve wisdom.

Chapter Two Outline

Section One: Kant and the Commands of Duty.

    I.   Kant and the problem of morality.

    II.   Morality and knowledge of right and wrong.

    III. Morality and proof.

Section Two: Three Reasons to Think About Ethics.

    I.   Proof of moral principles.

    II.   Doing the right thing.

    III. The "good life."

Section Three: Ethical Disagreements and the Categorical Imperative.

    I.   Three approaches.

        A.   The denial of variations.
        B.   The denial of objective, universal norms.
           1.   Ethical skepticism.
           2.   Ethical relativism.
        C.   The acknowledgement of variations.

    II.   The system of Kant.

        A.   Three basic elements of his system.
           1.   Individuals are rational beings.
           2.   Individuals have intrinsic worth.
           3.   Individuals are the authors of moral law.
        B.   The categorical imperative.

Section Four: Utilitarianism and the Calculation of Pleasures and Pain.

    I.   Bentham - the founder of utilitarianism.

        A.   The principle of utility.
        B.   The equation of happiness with pleasure.

    II.   The application of utilitarianism.

        A.   The hedonic calculus.
        B.   The greatest happiness principle.

III. Objections to utilitarianism.

    A.   The ambiguity of maximizing pleasure.
    B.   The pain of the few versus the pleasure of the greater number.
    C.   The justification of morally wrong acts.

*Ethics

The branch of philosophy which studies morality; the study of how one ought to act, of how moral value judgments are made.

Morals

This term is frequently used as a synonym for ethics. However, in philosophy, the term ethics denotes an area of philosophy. The term morals is often used to refer to a person's principles concerning what is right or wrong.

Good Life

A term used by the early Greeks to refer to how one should live life. For Plato, it consists of the harmony of the elements of the soul or self.

*Ethical Relativism

The view that moral principles vary from individual to individual, from culture to culture. It denies the existence of universal, objective moral principles.

Ethical Skepticism

The view that there can be no certainty about moral principles; also, the claim that moral terms are meaningless.

Norm

A standard of behavior; a rule or principle which is used to evaluate behavior as moral or immoral.

*Categorical Imperative

The moral principle of Immanuel Kant which is used to determine the individual's duty. The principle is this: act only according to that maxim by which you can at the same time will that it should become a universal law.

Utilitarianism

The moral (and social) theory developed by Jeremy Bentham which states that individuals should act in such a way that their actions result in the greatest good for the greatest number.

*Identity Crisis   An emotional period usually experienced during early adulthood or late adolescence in which there are uncertainties about life and what one should be doing.

Check List of Important Items

TERMS

Ethics
Ethical relativism
Good life
Autonomous
Identity crisis
Greatest Happiness principle

Categorical imperative
Utilitarianism
Ethical Skepticism
End-in-itself
Principle of utility
Ego integrity

THINKERS

Immanuel Kant
Ruth Benedict
Plato

Jeremy Bentham
David Hume
Erik Erikson

WRITINGS

Anthropology and the Abnormal

Groundwork of the Metaphysics of Morals

An Introduction to the Principles of Morals and Legislation

Republic

SELF TEST I

1.   For Immanuel Kant which of the following is the central question of morality? 1. what should I do? 2. how can I do what I know to be right? 3. which actions are immoral? 4. what is the good life?

2.   The founder of the moral theory of utilitarianism was _____.

3. David Hume has argued that human behavior is the result of our desires, that desires are really what move us to act. Kant disputes this claim and argues that _____ is the basis or should be the basis of our behavior.

4. Which of the following claims that there are no universal, objective moral principles? 1. Jeremy Bentham 2. Plato 3. ethical relativism 4. utilitarianism.

5. Bentham claims that one should base one's actions out of consideration for the greatest good for the greatest number. The term good is used by Bentham as synonymous with 1. the good life 2. physical well being 3. psychical well being 4. pleasure.

6. He is the contemporary thinker who uses the concept of ego integrity in his discussion of the good life.
   _____

7. This is a major dialogue of Plato that Wolff uses to illustrate Plato's theory of the self or soul.
   _____

8. Wolff presents this thinker as one of the strongest opponents to ethical relativism. 1. Kant 2. Bentham 3. Plato 4. Erikson.

9. This position denies that one can have any certainty about moral issues. 1. ethical objectivism 2. utilitarianism 3. ethical skepticism 4. Erikson's theory.

10. This thinker, who is an anthropologist, is a proponent of ethical relativism. _____.

11. One of the main premises of morality for Immanuel Kant concerns a value that must be placed on individuals. For Kant, man must be regarded as 1. having an intrinsic value 2. a means to an end 3. having an extrinsic value 4. having only relative value, since some people are simply worth more than others.

12. For Plato, the good life is the result of a certain balance of the elements of the soul or self. Which of the following is the major element in this balance? 1. the spirited element 2. the desires 3. the appetites 4. reason.

13. Wolff states that Kant was a student of the new science of his day. Did Kant see any conflict between science and ethics? 1. yes 2. no.

14. Which theory of ethics is presented as one which can be used to answer the hard questions of morality; those dilemmas where one does not really know what to do? 1. Kant's theory 2. ethical relativism 3. Plato's theory 4. utilitarianism.

15. Is there any relationship between the elements of the individual's soul and elements of society for Plato? 1. yes 2. no.

SELF TEST II

1. List and briefly explain the three reasons for studying ethics which Wolff discusses in section II.

2. What are the three elements of the soul according to Plato and how are they related to one another?

3. State Kant's categorical imperative in your own words and explain what you think it means.

4. What is basic moral principle of utilitarianism?

5. Kant's moral theory is composed of three major elements. List these and briefly discuss each one.

6. Discuss some of the objections which Wolff raises against utilitarianism.

7. What is Erikson's view of the good life?

8. Wolff discusses some strong points to utilitarianism. What are they? Do you think that they outweigh the objections that were presented?

9. What are some objections that could be leveled against Kant's system of morality?

10. List the three positions that thinkers have taken with respect to the variations of morals that exist from culture to culture or within a culture.

Chapter Three

Social Philosophy

Study Suggestions

In your study of philosophy, by now, you may have begun to realize that philosophy can be characterized by the kinds of questions that thinkers ask. One way to approach the material in this chapter then is to begin with a representative philosophical question that might be asked concerning society and then to see how the question is answered. One fundamental question that characterizes social philosophy is the following: What is the basic purpose or function of society? As you read through the chapter, look for the answer to this question which is given first by utilitarianism, then by the conservatives, and lastly, by socialists like Karl Marx. Also, be sure you take note of the various criticism which Wolff discusses for each of the three social theories.

Chapter Overview

This chapter deals with the area of philosophy called social philosophy or sometimes social-political philosophy, since the two are intimately related. There are three social theories which are examined here, and these are listed below:
1.   The utilitarianism of Bentham and Mill.
2.   The conservative view of society with Oakeshott and Tocquevill as representatives.
3.   The socialist views of Karl Marx and Marcuse.
Utilitarianism is discussed first and then the conservative and socialist positions are presented as reactions to Bentham and Mill.

Chapter Analysis

Section I

The first several paragraphs of section I give biographical information on John Stuart Mill. As you have seen in the last chapter with Kant, it is important to have some understanding of the life of a philosopher in order to more fully understand his theories. So you find that Mill's passionate concern for social reform was the direct result of his upbringing.

Next, Professor Wolff presents some of the major elements of Bentham's position of utilitarianism. You recall that utilitarianism was discussed in the last chapter as a moral theory but here it is presented as a social theory. This may seem to be some kind of inconsistency, but if you understand utilitarianism, first of all, as being a social-political theory that has a moral element, it may make more sense. Below is a summary of the main premises of utilitarianism:

1. The only good is pleasure and the only evil is pain with no qualitative differences. (this is the moral element)
2. All persons seek to satisfy their desires to the fullest in the most efficient manner. (this is the psychological element)
3. Education would eliminate superstition and ignorance and produce an enlightened citizenry. (this is the educational element)
4. Capitalism is the practice of the principle of utility and therefore, produces the greatest good for the greatest number. (this is the economic element)

For Bentham one of the basic purposes of society is to provide the conditions under which there would be produced the greatest happiness (pleasure) for the greatest number. His belief was that if the four above elements were present, then at least this one basic purpose of society would be fulfilled.

As you know from reading the text, Mill was at first a vigorous defender of utilitarianism but came to differ with Bentham in some important ways. Professor Wolff discusses these beginning with the second paragraph following the Adam Smith selection. Below is a summary of the three ways.

1.   Bentham emphasized the quantity aspect of pleasure, and Mill focused on the qualitative element of pleasure.

2.   Bentham believed that behavior was not affected by custom and habit, and therefore, could be calculated; whereas Mill argues the opposite - custom and habit do influence economic behavior and though it may be predictable, it is not calculable.

3.   Mill approves of some departures from the principle of laisser-faire, while Bentham does not; that is, for Mill, on some occasions the government would have the right of interference in private affairs.

For Mill, these revisions represent an attempt to make utilitarianism a more refined and consistent doctrine, and one that would be less subject to criticism. Neverless, there were intense criticisms from both the conservatives and the socialists.

Section II

Section II is a presentation of the criticisms of the conservatives. Wolff uses Oakeshott and Tocqueville to illustrate the conservative attack against utilitaritnism.

It is important to note that the conservative's criticisms are not a direct attack against utilitarianism but are directed against one of the basic presuppositions of their doctrine. In other words, the conservatives are not challenging whether society is productive of the greatest good for the greatest number, but rather they question the presupposition that man is a rational agent.

In the third paragraph in this section, Wolff discusses the two claims of the utilitarians regarding reason that are challenged by the conservatives. The claims are:

1.   It is reason thath determines the best means of satisfying the goals set by desire.
2.   Man is rational - he has the ability to deliberate, to evaluate alternatives, and to make decisions.

Oakeshott attacks claim number one by first critiquing what he understands to be the character and disposition of the rationalist. Although the first three paragraphs may appear to be only a listing of characteristics and dispositions of the rationalist, he no doubt is suggesting that these are undesirable traits. Notice the negative tone of Oakeshotts description here. In the last two paragraphs Oakeshotts makes the distinction between technical knowledge and practical knowledge. Technical knowledge is "susceptible of precise formulation" but practical knowledge is not. He then argues that the rationalist accepts technical knowledge but rejects practical knowledge thereby reducing all knowledge to technique, which he believes to be a fundamental mistake.

Claim number two listed above is discussed by Wolff in the several paragraphs following the Oakeshott selection. Two different conservative objections to reason are presented here. The first is that the conservatives deny that reason is the fundamental characteristic of humanity, and the second concerns the role of reason versus tradition. For the conservative, tradition rather than reason provides the superior guide for society. The Tocqueville selection is used to illustrate the conservative position on tradition.

Section III

This section presents the socialist reaction to utilitarianism or, more accurately, their reaction to capitalism which is the economic element of utilitarianism. You may want to refer to the brief summary of utilitarianism that was presented at the very beginning and take note of the fourth premise. This will show the relationship of Section III to utilitarianism.

Karl Marx, who is presented as the major critic of capitalism, maintains that it is not rational. Notice the implication of this claim. If Marx is correct, then utilitarianism which is emphasizing reason and the rational approach would contain a contradiction, and therefore, it would be an inconsistent doctrine. This would be a serious defect. Below is a summary of some of the main elements of Marx's position concerning the irrationality of capitalism:

1. Capitalism could not distribute efficiently the goods it produced.
2. The goods produced were not always the ones most in need.
3. High profits required low wages which thereby reduced the ability of the worker to buy the good being produced.

4.   Competition resulted in overproduction which in turn caused unemployment that would finally lead to depression and the repeat of the cycle.
5.   Capitalism produced a destructive alienation of labor.

Wolff presents a second critic of capitalism, Marcuse, who is a twentieth-century supporter of Marx's views.

Marcuse, like Marx, also attacks capitalism as being irrational in spite of the advances that workers have made in modern capitalistic societies. In the passage in the reading from Marcuse, notice how he focuses on society's concern of preventing an atomic war and argues that this concern obscures the underlying irrationality that exists. Here are some main points he makes in the passage to show the irrational nature of modern western societies:

1.   Our need to be protected leads to the production of a defense system which itself could lead to the destruction of the human race.
2.   Economic growth and individual well-being comes about as a result of expanding the defense system and this futher perpetuates the very danger society is trying to avoid.
3.   This kind of production " is destructive of the free development of human needs."
4.   Even if the majority accepts the idea of increased protection and the expansion of the defense system, this does not make the society rational.
5.   Majority acceptance is the result of their reasoning and desires being corrupted by the capitalistic system.

Keep in mind that Marcuse here is criticizing contemporary societies and not directly the overall social theory of utilitarianism. However, it is a criticism of the economic element of that theory, and point number five, above, does strike at the psychological element. This last element is discussed by Wolff in the last paragraphs in this section.

The last section of the chapter -Contemporary Application- is a consideration of a different philosophical question from the one raised at the beginning of this section of the Study Guide. There utilitarianism was viewed from the perspective of the goals or purposes of society. Here it is viewed from the perspective of how societal wealth should be distributed.

For utilitarianism the allocation of the goods of society is based on the free market, which is the application of the laissez-faire principle. For socialists like Marx, the allocation of goods is based on needs determined by the collective whole and not the ability to pay.

The Rand passage is a satire that attacks Marx's position. It is interesting to note in this passage that Rand suggests that the very process of providing for the needs of others involves a kind of contradiction- "the more you tried to live up to it, the more you suffered." The irony is that Marx has critcized capitalism for being irrational, and in his own system Rand points out a basic irrationality.

The Goodin passage is presented by Wolff as a contrast to Rand's views, but the passage also would challenge the utilitarian's theory concerning the wealth of society. Notice that Goodin is concerned with moral responsibility as it relates to the allocation of the goods of society. Compare this with the moral element of utilitarianism to see how his theory is a challenge to that view.

Chapter Three Outline

Section One: Mill and Classical Laissez-Faire Liberalism

I. The main elements of utilitarianism for Bentham and James Mill.

    A. The Moral element - the only good is pleasure and the only evil is pain.

    B. The Psychological element - people seek to satisfy their desires to the fullest in the most efficient manner.

    C. The Educational element - education would eliminate superstition and ignorance and produce an enlightened citizenry.

    D. The Economic element - capitalism produces the greatest good (happiness) for the greatest number.

II. The major differences between Bentham and Mill

    A. Bentham emphasizes quantity, whereas Mill emphasizes quality of pleasure.

    B. For Bentham, custom and habit are not factors of behavior whereas for Mill they are.

    C. Limited interference by the government is approved of by Mill but not by Bentham.

Section Two: The Conservative Attack on Capitalism

I. Two claims of utilitarianism regarding reason

    A. Reason determines the best means of satisfying the goals set by desires.
        1. Oakeshott's attack of this claim.

    B. Man is rational.
        1. Tocqueville's criticism of this claim.

Section Three: The Socialist Attack on Capitalism

I. The attack on the economic element of utilitarianism.

    A. Marx's arguments.
    B. Marcuse's arguments.

Section Four: Contemporary Application

I.   The distribution of the goods of society

    A.   Rand's position.
    B.   Goodin's position.

KEY TERMS

Utilitarianism | The view that society should be productive of the greatest good for the greatest number.

Rational | Based on or appealing to reason.

Irrational | Contrary to reason; involving a contradiction.

*Capitalism | The private ownership of business and industry that produce goods which are priced and marketed on the basis of supply and demand.

Argument | Reasoning involving a conclusion which is supported by premises.

*Laissez-faire | Limited government interference in the producing or marketing of the goods of society.

Liberal | A social-political view which emphasizes personal liberty and individual freedom rather than equality.

Conservative | A social-political view that emphasizes the status quo and custom or tradition.

*Marxism | The social-political view of Karl Marx which emphasizes individual equality.

*Alienation | The term used by Marx to describe the relation of the laborer to the product produced.

End | Used in the sense of a goal; having intrinsic value.

Means | The process or method used in achieving a goal; having extrinsic value.

*Socialism | The social-political theory wherein the members of society collectively own the resources and determine how they will be used.

Check List of Important Items

TERMS

Utilitarianism
Laissez-faire
Means of production
Social Philosophy
Alienation of Labor

Capitalism
Argumentt
Conservative
Socialism

Irrational
Liberal
Ends-means
rational

THINKERS

John Stuart Mill
James Mill
Adam Smith
Alexis de Tocqueville

Herbert Marcuse
Karl Marx
Michael Oakeshott

WRITINGS

The Wealth of Nations

Economic-Philosophic Manuscripts of 1844

Utilitarianism

The Principles of Political Economy

The Old Regime and the French Revolution

One-Dimensional Man

SELF TEST I

1. According utilitarism, the best judge of individual happiness is the impartial judge. True   False.

2. Tocqueville is presented as an advocate of which of these? (1) the liberal position (2) the conservative position (3) the Marxist position (4) the capitalist position.

3. The socialist attack on capitalism focuses on the irrationality issue. True   False.

4. One of the basic differences between Mill and Bentham concerns the concept of pleasure. For Bentham

37

pleasures differ _____ whereas for Mill they differ _____.

5. He is an advocate of Marx's social-political philosophy. (1) Oakeshott (2) Marcuse (3) Rand (4) Tocqueville.

6. Which of the following attack the view that reason is the best guide for human behavior? (1) socialists (2) liberals (3) conservatives (4) capitalists.

7. One of Marx's basic criticisms of capitalism involves which of the following? (1) the alienation of labor (2) the private ownership of the means of production (3) the making of profit (4) all of these.

8. Utilitarianism and socialism are compatible theories. True False.

9. This is a main element of capitalism. (1) laissez-faire (2) custom and tradition (3) the collective ownership of the means of production (4) all of these.

10. The welfare state is a reference to Marx's social system. True False.

11. He was the founder of utilitarianism. _____

12. This individual's theory is responsible for the economic element of utilitarianism. 1. Adam Smith 2. James Mill 3. Karl Marx 4. Marcuse.

13. Marx would agree with which of these? 1. that capitalism was unequaled at production 2. that capitalism was good at the distribution of goods 3. that capitalism produced shoddy goods 4. that capitalism created unfair competition in the market place.

14. According to Wolff, what is the primary target of the conservative attack on utilitarianism?
   _____

15. This thinker saw the elimination of the aristocracy as a threat to real freedom. 1. Marx 2. Tocqueville 3. Oakeshott 4. Burke.

SELF TEST II

1. List the four elements of utilitarianism and identify each; i.e., economic, moral, etc.

2. Discuss some of the criticisms that the conservatives level against utilitarianism.

3. What are some of the differences between Bentham and Mill on the theory of utilitarianism?

4. Explain what Marx means by the term alienation.

5. What did Marx think would be accomplished by a revolution?

6. Marcuse claims that individuals in societies like our own are really not free. Discuss what he means by this? What is Wolff's appraisal of his position?

7. Briefly discuss the criticism that capitalism is irrational. What does Marx mean by irrational?

8. What role did education play in society according to Bentham?

9. As you understand the social systems of utilitarianism and Marx's theory, which seems to you to be the best. Why?

10. Discuss how you would have society structured.

Chapter Four

Political Philosophy

Study Suggestions

The previous chapter on social philosophy has given you a good background for understanding most of this chapter. As was suggested earlier in the Study Guide, these two areas of philosophy are intimately related. In section I of this chapter, there are two main concepts that you must grasp. The first one is that of the "state" which Wolff explains as having two essential characteristics. Make sure, as you read the section, to get an understanding of these. The second most important concept to focus on is the "social contract." Again, get an understanding of it before you read on in the chapter. You will probably have the most difficulty in section III which covers Marx's theory. There are technical terms used that you may not be familiar with, so read carefully Wolff's explanation of these. The Study Guide's analysis should be of help to you in this section.

Chapter Overview

As the name of chapter indicates, the topic dealt with is the area of philosophy called political philosophy. There are three major political theories presented beginning with Rousseau's theory of the social contract. After a consideration of some problems with the theory, the second major political theory, Fascism, is examined. The chapter concludes with an discussion of Marx's doctrine which is called historical materialism.

Chapter Analysis

Section I

The first three paragraphs of this section give you a brief biographical sketch of Rousseau's life. It is interesting to note the sharp contrast between between the life styles of Kant and Rousseau. Following paragraphs introduce the first of some fundamental political concepts - the state. Here, Wolff, defines the state as "whoever makes the laws, gives the commands, and enforces them on everyone living within" a certain area. The following two characteristics of the state are then explained:

1.   States exercise some kind of force or the threat of force to get their subjects to obey.
2.   States claim that they have the right to be obeyed; that they are legitimate.

Of these two, the second one is the most important, and you will find several paragraphs devoted to an analysis of it. It deals with issue of the "right to rule," and one of the points that Wolff makes concerning it is that most people in societies believe this claim and obey even when they are not forced to. He notes that people may obey from habit, but the underlying reason is the belief in the legitimacy of the state.

Next, the fundamental question of political philosophy is raised from several perspectives. The important point here is to get a grasp of what the question is no matter the perspective or how the question is asked. The question basically comes down to this: when is the claim of the right to rule a valid claim? Here you must distinguish the claim from those who make the claim. So, the focus of political philosophy is on whoever is making the claim, and the question might be better understood in this way: Why should one accept the state's claim of the right to rule? There is a brief discussion of the ancient and medieval view of the legitimacy of the state followed by the sixteenth and seventeenth century views. The legitimacy of the state for eighteenth century thinkers includes the element of autonomy. Therefore, in Rousseau's time the fundamental question comes to this: Can one be free while at the same time submitting to the laws of a legitimate state?

Rousseau's solution is based on the concept of the "social contract" which is another term that you must understand in order to have some real insight into his system. Your understanding of the nature of a contract from law, as a binding, voluntary agreement between two or more parties, should help you to understand what Rousseau is saying. The two parties to the "social" contract are "the citizen and all the other members of society." The state formed on the basis of the social contract is legitimate; that is, it can demand compliance from its citizens to its laws, since they have voluntarily agreed to obey them as part of the contract. Also, the state demands conpliance because the citizens receive certain benefits from being party to the contract, and hence, must carry out their end of the bargin. The autonomy issue may be harder to understand. The idea is this: when you and others freely submit to being ruled by the state, you are claiming that your will is now the same as the commonweal, and when you obey the state, you are, in fact, acting in conformity with your own will. This may strike you as an odd concept of autonomy or freedom but do not confuse not understanding a concept or idea with not accepting the concept or idea. Try to do the former before you do the latter.

Two basic problems for Rousseau's theory are examined next. They are: 1.   How can everyone participate in the making of laws?
           2.   How can laws be made when there is disagreement about what the laws should be?
The first problem is handled by Rousseau's insisting that the state be kept small enough for everyone to participate. The second problem is addressed in the third reading from <u>The Social Contract</u>. The essence of Rousseau's argument is that the minority are bound to the majority position as a consequence of the original contract, and further, that the issue is not that of the lack of consent on the part of the minority. "The citizens consent to all the laws," claims Rousseau, because they are enacted on the notion of being conformable to the general will, which is their will. To be in the minority is to have made a mistake in judgment as to what the general will really was. Rousseau's argument here is invalid, so be sure to read the following material in Wolff to know why.

Wolff discusses two major criticisms of the social contract theory in the remainder of section I. A summary of the two follows:
     1.   With the exception of the United States, no other societies have actually come into being in the way that Rousseau's theory states.
     2.   The social contract would not seem to be binding on those future members of society who were not a party to the original contract.

The first criticism was raised by David Hume, and the selected passage illustrates the nature of this attack. Philosophers, like John Locke, who support the contract theory, have a reply to the second criticism based on the concept of "tacit consent." The idea amounts to this: a person through his behavior can embark on an agreement to do certain things that is just as binding as if they were written down. One early and well known instance of this notion of tacit consent occurs in the <u>Crito</u>, a Platonic dialogue that describes a prison visit of Crito who is a close friend of Socrates. Crito is attempting to persuade Socrates to escape from prison, and Socrates explains why the escape would be unjust. His reasoning is that he has bound himself to the laws of Athens (meaning that he has an obligation to obey them) more than others because he has through his behavior of living in Athens for seventy years given his consent to abide by the laws. Even though Soctates had no hand in formulating the laws, he argues that they are, nevertheless, binding; his living in Athens under the laws constitutes his consent to be governed by those laws. Socrates, like Locke, maintained that one was always free to leave a society whose laws seemed to be unjust. This latter point represents the weakness of the tacit consent argument, since today it is not as easy to leave a society as it was in Socrates' or Locke's day.

Section II

Section II of this chapter begins with an examination of additional anticontract criticisms. The Burke reading contains the argument that the state cannot be regarded merely as a contractual arrangement; to do so is to misunderstand the essence of what the state is. This view of society is what Wolff discusses as the organic theory in the next several paragraphs.

The main feature of this view of society is the emphasis on the good of the whole -the state- rather than that of the individual citizen. According to Wolff, the basic principle of the organic state is "sacrifice for the good of the state, not self-interested calculation of personal advantage." The state becomes something more than a collection of individuals living together for some common good.

If you will turn to section IV in chapter two, to the Bentham reading, you will find the important contrast between the liberal view of the state and this organic view. Notice Bentham's description of the community -you can substitute state or society for community- as "a fictitious body, composed of individual persons who are considered as constituting as it were its members." So the difference between the liberal view and the organic view of the state comes down to this: the good of the individual versus the good of the state.

The last part of section II is the presentation of fascism as an illustration of the organic view. As you read this selection, notice the very clear preeminence given the state.

Section III

The last section of this chapter, section III, is the examination of a third political philosophy, that of Karl Marx. In the second paragraph, Wolff lists three elements of Marx's historical materialism, two of which will be further examined in this section. The three elements are:
    1. A theory of human nature.
    2. A theory of how society is organized.
    3. A theory of how societies develop and change.
The first element was presented in the previous chapter, so there is no further discussion of it here.

The most important concept to grasp in understanding Marx's theory of the organization of society -the second element- is that of the "material base." This term is used to refer to the economically productive activities of persons in securing food, shelter, and the other necessities of life. There are three elements that constitute the material base:
    1. The means of production.
    2. The forces of production.
    3. The social relationships of production.

The first two elements are briefly, but clearly, explained in the fifth paragraph and the next three paragraphs are devoted to an exposition of the last element, which Wolff says is the most important. If you will think in terms of classes -the class of workers and the class of owners- as you read or reread these paragraphs, I think that you will see what Marx means by the social ralationships of production.

Pay attention to Wolff's description of how there come to be classes according to Marx and also, to why the classes are accepted as legitimate by later generations. So the social relationships of production involve the various social, economic interactions   between the class of workers and the class of owners.

For Marx, there is another kind of relationship that exists in the structure of society; that between the substructure, which is the material base, and the superstructure. You could think of the superstructure as composed of nonmaterial things like laws, religion, art, and philosophy. His theory is that the material order causes the fundamental ideas contained in these areas. This is really an important point is his theory, and notice, that it is the reversal of how we usually conceive of things as happening. Rather than our ideas being the cause of some material order, for Marx, they are the **result** of the material order! You must remember that Marx is adopting the philosophical position called materialism - the view that ultimate reality consists only of material entities. This is why the material base is of primary importance and the superstructure is secondary, and indeed, dependent on the substructure.

Thus, even the state is the result of a particular material order. Remember the term "capitalism" from the previous chapter; for Marx, this is one of the stages of history in which the dominant factor of production is capital or really the ownership of factories. This kind of material order will be the cause of a system of government (a state) that will favor the owners rather than the workers. Wolff gives an interesting historical sketch of how even some important philosophers have developed philosophical systems that just happen to coincide with the interests of prevailing class.

Finally, we come to the last element in the overall political theory of Marx, that of social change. What Wolff is explaining in these last several paragraphs has to do with Marx's analysis of various stages or phases of history. I believe you will have a better understanding of this section if you have some brief knowledge of what they are. Here is a list of the five in the <u>order</u> that they develop:
1. Primitive communal: people living in small groups where material goods are shared; no classes exist.
2. Slavery: the basic means of production is people; classes exist -slave owners and slaves.
3. Feudalism: the basic means of production is land; classes still exist -land owners and land workers.
4. Capitalism: the basic means of production is capital; the two classes

		are the owners and the workers.
5.	Communism:	all people collectively own everything; no classes and no state.

The very brief description following each term in the list is only intended to give you a general idea of the essential features of each stage of history.

Part of Marx's ploitical theory, then, has to do with why these stages come about as they do. For him, each stage of history is marked by "class conflict," and this results in a synthesis, that is, the emergence of a new stage of history. Only in the last stage are there no classes, and hence, no class conflict and no need for the state. This is what Wolff is discussing in this section of the chapter under the topic of social changes.

Chapter Four Outline

Section One: Rousseau and the Theory of the Social
                Contract

I.   The life of reason.

II.   The nature of the state.
      A.   The state defined.
      B.   The characteristics of the state.
            1.   The element of obedience.
            2.   The right to rule.
      C.   The acceptance of the right to rule.

III. The legitimacy of the state.
      A.   The citizen's obligation.
            1.   Ancient, Medieval times.
            2.   Sixteenth and seventeenth centuries.
            3.   The period of the enlightenment.
      B.   Rousseau's answer.
            1.   The social contract.
            2.   Autonomy and freedom.
      C.   Two problems for Rousseau's theory.
            1.   Individual participation in the
                  government.
            2.   Decisions when there is disagreement.
      D.   Hume's criticisms.
      E.   Locke's theory of tacit consent.

Section Two: Fascism and the Organic State

I.   Burke's criticism of the contract theory.
      A.   The organic view of the state.
            1.   The subordination of the parts.
            2.   The good of the whole.
            3.   The role of traditions.
      B.   The effect of major historical events.

II.   The disruption of political and social unity.
      A.   Social-economic change.
      B.   Wars.

III. The objection of liberalism.
      A.   The search for new unity.
      B.   The rise of fascism.
            1.   The elements of fascism.
            2.   Mussolini.

Section Three: Marx's Theory of the State

I.   Three elements of historical materialism.

A.   Human nature.
B.   Social and economic organization.
      1.   The material base.
            a.   Means of production.
            b.   The forces of production.
            c.   The social relationships of
                  production.
      2.   The division of labor.
      3.   The superstructure of society.
            a.   The role of the state.
            b.   The character of the state.
C.   Social change.
      1.   The class structure.
      2.   Class conflict.
      3.   The "withering away" of the state.
      4.   Revolutions.

Political philosophy — The branch of philosophy that is concerned with the study of the nature of the state.

State — The collection of those who construct, issue, and enforce laws on others living within a given area.

Anarchist — One who denies that the state has the right to rule; the denial of the legitimacy of the state.

*Social contract — A concept used by political philosophers to explain the legitimacy of the state; it is a voluntary and binding agreement between an individual and others to accept certain social-political conditions as a basis for the common good of all.

Tacit consent — A term used to explain how later generations of citizens become parties to the social contract; the idea that a person through his behavior has given his word to obey certain principles or laws.

*Fascism — The political theory of Mussolini; an organic view of the state in which the supreme value is placed on the state rather than on the individual. The individual exists for the good of the state.

Historical materialism — The name of Marx's political theory which analyzes human nature, the sturcture of social order, and how societies on the basis of these elements change over time.

Material base — A term used by Marx to refer to the segment of society which produces the basic necessities of life; it consists of the means of production, the factors of

	production, and the social relationships of production.
Superstructure	A Marxian term which refers to the nonmaterial or secondary elements of society like law, art, religion, and philosophy. These elements are the result of the material order that exists.
*Proletariat	Marx and Engels use this term to refer to the worker or the members of the working class.
*Bourgeoisie	Those who own the means of production; the dominant class at the capitalistic stage of history.

Check List of Important Items

TERMS

Political Philosophy
State
Legitimate
Superstructure
Material base
Forces of Production
Historical Materialism
Division of Labor
Social relationships of production

Social contract
Anarchist
Teleological
Fascism
Tacit consent
Proletariat
Means of Production
Liberal theory
Alienation

THINKERS

Jean-Jacques Rousseau
David Hume
John Locke
Edmund Burke

Benito Mussolini
Karl Marx
Friedrich Engels

WRITINGS

The Social Contract

Of the Original Contract

Second Treatise of Government

Reflections of the French Revolution

<u>The Doctrine of Fascism</u>

<u>The Communist Manifesto</u>

<u>Herr Eugen Duhring's Revolution in Science</u>

SELF TEST I

1. According to Rousseau, the legitimacy of the state is based on which of these? 1. Divine revelation 2. the social contract 3. tacit consent 4. social tradition.

2. This position elevates the state above the individual and perhaps at the expense of the individual. _____.

3. Which of these thinkers does Wolff discuss as being an opponent of the contract theory? 1. Burke 2. Locke 3. Rousseau 4. Bentham.

4. In Marx's political theory, there are three elements of the material base of society. Which of the three does Wolff say is the most important? _____.

5. One of the problems that was raised with Rousseeau's social contract theory was which of these? 1. the problem of determining who would rule society 2. the problem of making decisions when there are disagreements 3. the problem of the right to rule 4. the problem of getting individuals to obey the laws.

6. The organic view of the state best describes the political philosophy of this thinker. 1. Locke 2. Marx 3. Mussolini 4. Engels.

7. According to Wolff, most philosophers attempt to explain or define the state teleologically. 1. true 2. false.

8. This doctrine denies the legitimacy of the state, the state's right to rule. _____

9. Which of the following claims that the state would eventually become unnecessary? 1. Locke 2. Hume 3. Mussolini 4. Marx.

10. Wolff claims that all states, no matter what their purpose is, have two fundamental characteristics. Is one of these that they use force to secure obedience to their laws? 1. yes 2. no.

11. According to the text, the fundamental question of political philosophy is which of these? 1. What is the good life? 2. When is the state legitimate? 3. What form or structure should be the basis of society? 4. Should the state or the individual have supreme importance?

12. Of the political theories presented in this chapter, only one affiliates itself with religion. Which of the following does this? 1. Fascism 2. Hume's theory 3. Historical materialism 4. the social contract theory.

13. This is the term Marx and Engels use to refer to the class of workers.

    _____

14. David Hume was presented as an opponent to the contract theory. Which of the following is his objection to the concept of the social contract? 1. that no society ever came into existence on the basis of a contract 2. that it would be impossible to get the majority of people to agree to the conditions of a contract 3. that future generations would not be bound to the contract 4. that such a contract would be voluntary for most individuals.

15. For Marx, individuals are considered as socially productive and develop such methods as the division of labor and systems of exchange in order to live. Does he believe that this type of cooperation leads to the equitable distribution of goods and brings about a kind of equality in a capitalistic society? 1. yes 2. no.

SELF TEST II

1. Briefly explain the two main characteristics of the state.

2. How does the social contract explain the legitimacy of the state?

3. What does Marx mean by the social relationships of production and what role does this concept play in his political theory?

4. Explain the concept of "tacit consent" and why it is used by political philosophers like John Locke.

5. List and briefly describe some of the main elements of Mussolini's fascism.

6. What is meant by the organic view of the state? List some thinkers who are advocates of this position.

7. What role does revolution play in Marx's political theory? Relate this to the Wolff's analysis of Marx's theory as consisting of three parts.

8. How is the AIDS issue related to the issues of political philosophy that have been presented in this chapter?

9. Discuss some of the objections that thinkers like Hume and Burke direct against the social contract theory.

10. What do you see as objections to Marx's political theory?

Chapter Five

Philosophy of Art

Study Suggestions

As you read chapter five, keep in mind that art is being
discussed in a broad sense that includes many different
forms and not merely painting. Note that many of the
selected readings deal with art in the literary form. In
section I, the major concept you need understand is the
"appearance-reality" distinction. Wolff presents several
examples to clarify how the concept is being used. Section
II should give you little difficulty . In section III, the
basic concept to know is another distinction; in this
case,a value distinction between instrumental and intrinsic
values. You may want to refer to chapter two of the study
guide where this distinction was introduced in explaining
the moral theory of Immanuel Kant. The most difficult
section of this chapter is the last one which deals with
the theory of Marcuse. There are some psychological terms
like "necessary repression," "surplus repression," and,
"transcendence" which you need to know in order to have
some idea of his concept of art.

Chapter Overview

This chapter is an examination of six different views or
conceptions of art. What follows is a list of the
representatives and a brief description of their views:
1.   Plato - a critic of art who claims that art is a
distortion of reality.

2. Aristotle - a defender of art because of its useful consequences or its instrumental value.
3. Wilde - a defender of art on the basis of its intrinsic value.
4. Wordsworth - he is an example of the romantic conception of art.
5. Tolstoy - a defender of the religious dimension of art.
6. Marcuse - he advocates the negative function of art.

Chapter Analysis

Section I

This contains the presentation of Plato as a great literary artist as well as an important critic of art. First, Wolff discusses three elements which make Plato's dialogues works of art:
1. They present genuine arguments that are persuasive.
2. They contain realistic characters.
3. The personalities and speech of the characters exemplifies "the philosophical theories he is trying to expound."

Then, in the fifth paragraph, Wolff introduces the basic metaphysical distinction which Plato uses in his criticism of art - this is the distinction between how things appear as opposed to how they really are. The concept in not a difficult one to grasp, and there are several examples presented to illustrate it. Note this important point: one of the main prerequisites of applying the distinction is the possession of certain knowledge or wisdom. In the Gorgias example, Wolff shows how Plato develops the characters of Gorgias, Polus, and Callicles as individuals whose personalities mirror the philosophical positions they each espouse. According to Wolff, Plato intends "the dramatic persuasiveness of his characters -their appearance- to reveal, rather than conceal, the truth about their souls -their reality." One of the paradoxes of Plato's dialogues, Wolff argues, is that because of their artistic character one could be lead away from the message they contain.

The last several paragraphs reveal Plato's specific objections to art which are based on the appearance-reality distinction. For Plato, art deals with appearances only, and therefore, leads to a false view of reality. It is to be condemned on this basis, and further, Plato argues, it disrupts the inner harmony of the soul. Recall from chapter two, Plato's theory of the soul involving a harmony of three elements -reason, the appetites and desires, and the spirited element. The harmony consisted of reason being in control of the other two elements, and it is this loss of control by reason which art produces.

Section II

In this section, Wolff presents Aristotle as a defender of art in opposition to Plato's two criticisms. After the first two paragraphs which give you some background information on the life of Aristotle, you will find a discussion of Aristotle's position. In order to understand his rebuttal of Plato's criticism, you need to get a clear idea of the difference between their metaphysical views. Below is a summary of their views of reality.

Reality for Plato: It consists of nonphysical entities called forms or ideas. Physical objects exist but are not real and are imitations of the forms. For example, a particular physical object might approximate (Plato uses the expression "participate in ") the form beauty, but is not itself beauty. Thus, beauty can only be apprehended with the mind, not the senses. Physical objects are appearances and to mistake them for reality is to be ignorant of the true nature of reality. Since artists deal with images of physical objects, their focus is twice removed from reality.

Reality for Aristotle   It consists of physical objects and not transcendental entities like forms. Form and matter exist together, not separately. Beauty, for example, can be understood through the use of observation coupled with reason; it exists in particular objects and cannot be divorced from them.

Aristotle's objection to Plato stems from this difference as to the nature of reality. Since reality is physical, then works of art that reflect physical things focus one's attention on reality and not merely on appearances.

Aristotle's rebuttal of Plato second objection rests on what Wolff describes as a psychological point. His rebuttal simply amounts to a denial of Plato's claim that art disrupts the harmony of the soul. Aristotle's position, as summarized by Wolff, is that "those harmful passions are present anyway, far better to release them in the controlled setting of the drama than to bottle them up." So, the value of art for Aristotle is in the dissipation of certain feelings or emotions, and thus, art would not result in the destruction of the inner harmony of the soul.

Section III

The view of art examined in this section is expressed in the phrase "art for art's sake." The basic idea is that art has value in and of itself and not as a means to some end. Wolff spends several paragraphs explaining the fundamental distinction which is used to state the above position, so be sure you understand the difference between instrumental and intrinsic values. Below is a summary of the two.

1. Instrumental value   a thing (not just material things) has value as a means to some end; it is not valued merely for itself.
2. Intrinsic value   a thing has inner worth; it is valued for itself without considering the consequences of its use.

The Wilde selection is used to illustrate this view of art - that art has intrinsic value.

Section IV

Romanticism is the view of art discussed in this section. The first paragraph presents neoclassicism as a traditional approach to art that is the focus of the romantic rebellion. This traditional view emphasized reason and certain objective principles as basic guidelines for art. The romantic view challenges both of these neoclassic tenets. Creative imagination is exalted above reason and is the primary source of our insights into reality. Likewise, the subjective feelings or emotions of the artist become the ground of truth and knowledge. In the Wordsworth reading, the art form of poetry is discussed from the romantic view of art.

Section V

Tolstoy is another example of the instrumental approach to art but what differentiates him from the others that have thus far been presented is his emphasis on the religious dimension of art. According to Wolff, Tolstoy sees art as one of two fundamental ways of communication, the other is speech. It is feeling that art communicates, and this, for Tolstoy, is one of the functions or purposes of art. Some important elements of art are the following:

1. It should generate intensity (infectiousness) of feelings which unite people and this depends on the sincerity of the artist.
2. It must deal with commonplace things which most individuals can relate to.
3. It must transmit religious feeling.

This last element is the most important one for Tolstoy because religious feeling is one of the things that unite all individuals. Since this is also a function of art, it must include what he calls a religious perception. The reading clearly reveals Tolstoy's religious element.

Section VI

As was mentioned in the Study Suggestions, I think that this is the most difficult section in the chapter, and I hope you have read it at least a couple of times.

For Marcuse, art has a negative element and it is this which makes art of value. Wolff spends several paragraphs on Marcuse's revision of Freudian theory. First, beginning in the third paragraph, there is an explanation of the development of the "unconscious" in which there is the repression of strong desires, feelings, etc. The two features of the unconscious are:

1. It is timeless; for example, repressed feelings may surface years or decades later in one's life.
2. Its content has an ambivalent character; part of the self hates what it represses, but another part of the self lusts after the repressed.

This repression which, in a sense, is stored in the unconscious is a necessary foundation of civilization and exists in two forms: necessary and surplus. Necessary repression is that which is essential for survival - Wolff gives some examples to illustrate it. Surplus repression is that which is not really required by the conditions of reality, but is forced on individuals by those who are in dominant positions. It is this surplus repression, Marcuse argues, that must be eliminated and one of the functions of art is to accomplish this. Specifically, art forms that are in opposition to established norms that involve surplus repression are to be employed. So this negative element of art -the rebellion against certain norms- is what brings about a reduction in surplus repression and, consequently, gives value to art. Notice the extreme contrast between Wilde's view of art and Marcuse's with his emphasis on its social function.

Chapter Five Outline

Section One: Plato's Attack on the Poets

    I.   Plato as an artist.
        A.   The artistic elements of his dialogues.
            1.   Genuine arguments.
            2.   Realistic characters.
            3.   The exemplification of his theories.
        B.   The "appearance-reality" distinction.
        C.   The nature of knowledge.

    II.   The Gorgias.
        A.   The personalities of the characters.
        B.   The arguments of the characters.

    III. Plato's criticism of Art.
        A.   Two basic questions.
        B.   The criticism in the Republic.
        C.   The paradox of the singer.

Section Two: Aristotle's Defense of the Poets

    I.   Background on Aristotle.
        A.   Aristotle as a student of Plato.
        B.   Aristotle as teacher.

    II.   Aristotle's defense of art.
        A.   Plato vs. Aristotle on the nature of art.
        B.   The metaphysical disagreement.
            1.   Plato's theory of forms.
            2.   Aristotle's objections.
        C.   The psychological element.
        D.   Contemporary concerns.

    III. The Poetics.

Section Three: Art for Art's Sake

    I.   A distinction of values.
        A.   Instrumental values.
        B.   Intrinsic values.

    II.   Art as intrinsic value.

    III. Oscar Wilde reading.

Section Four: Romanticism

I.   Neoclassicism vs. romanticism.

II. The romantic rebellion.
     A.   The role of reason.
     B.   The role of knowledge.

III. Wordsworth reading.

Section Five: Tolstoy's Religious Defense of Art

I.   Art and instrumental value.
     A.   The romantic conception.
     B.   Tolstoy's view.

II. Two means of communication.
     A.   Speech.
     B.   Art.

III. The nature of art.
     A.   The role of sincerity.
     B.   The element of universality.
     C.   The religious dimension.

IV. Tolstoy readings.

Section Six: Marcuse and the Uses of Art

I.   The different conceptions of art.

II. Marcuse's view.

III. Marcuse's use of Freud's theory.
     A.   The nature of unconscious.
          1.   The temporal character.
          2.   It's ambivalence.
     B.   The role of repression.
          1.   Necessary repression.
          2.   Surplus repression.

IV. The Social function of art.
     A.   Art and the elimination of surplus repression.
     B.   Art and escape.

V.   Marcuse reading.

. Appearance

A metaphysical term which refers to how things seem to be as opposed to how they really are.

· Reality

How thing are in and of themselves as opposed to how they seem to be. (note: these first two terms are usually used together as an important metaphysical distinction)

. *Metaphysics

The branch of philosophy that studies the question of what is real; the study of the nature of reality.

. Forms

A metaphysical term used by Plato to refer to non-material, eternal, and changeless entities that constitute reality. Examples of forms are beauty, justice, man, etc.

. *Instrumental value

The worth that something has due to its use. For many, education has an instrumental value because it is a means to an end; it is not viewed as having any inherent worth.

. *Intrinsic value

The inherent worth that something has. For some, education is valued for the sake of itself and not as a means to some end; it has intrinsic value.

Aesthetics

The branch of philosophy that deals with the study of beauty. Philosophy of art is used as a synonymous term for aesthetics.

Neoclassicism

The theory of art that emphasized "order, proportion, reason," and objective principles.

*Romanticism

The late eighteenth movement which rebelled against the elements of neoclassicism; it emphasized creative imagination and subjectivity as the basis of truth in art.

*Repression	A Freudian term which refers to a mental regulation of strong desires, thoughts, and ideas that are considered anti-social.
Necessary Repression	The suppression of certain desires, feelings, and thoughts in order to survive at a given stage of society.
Surplus Repression	The excess or unnecessary suppression of desires that is the result of the domination of those in power.

Check List of Important Items

TERMS

Philosophy of Art
Appearance-reality
Instrumental value
Necessary repression

Intrinsic value
Neoclassicism
Metaphysics
Surplus Repression

Dialogue
Romanticism
Transcendence
Aesthetics

THINKERS

Plato
Aristotle
Oscar Wilde
William Wordsworth

Gorgias
Leo Tolstoy
Sigmund Freud
Herbert Marcuse

WRITINGS

Republic

The Poetics

Intentions

Preface to the Lyrical Ballads

What is Art?

One-Dimensonal Man

SELF TEST I

1. The romantic movement in art places more emphasis on _____ rather than on reason.

2. These thinkers both see art as involving a negative element. 1. Plato and Aristotle 2. Wilde and Wordsworth 3. Marcuse and Tolstoy 4. Plato and Marcuse.

3. According to Wolff, is Aristotle considered a great literary artist as was Plato? 1. yes 2. no.

4. This is the kind of value that underlies the expression "art for art's sake." 1. innate 2. instrumental 3. subjective 4. intrinsic.

5. A large portion of his theory of art is based on Freudian theory. 1. Tolstoy 2. Marcuse 3. Wilde 4. Wordsworth.

6. Which of the following is one of the major objections that Plato raises about art? 1. it lacks a religious dimension 2. it causes a disruption to the inner harmony of the soul 3. it takes time away from more important subjects like mathematics or philosophy 4. it tends to be anti-social and therefore is a threat to well ordered societies.

7. Plato and Aristotle are presented as taking opposite positions regarding the value of art. According to Wolff, the basis of their disagreement concerns which of these? 1. a difference of metaphysical views 2. a difference of religious views 3. a difference of social views 4. a difference of political views.

8. With which of the following statements would Tolstoy most likely agree? 1. great art relies on specialized talent and skill 2. great art is of commonplace things 3. an appreciation of art exists only for those who have cultivated tastes. 4. art has primarily an intrinsic rather than an instrumental value.

9. For Marcuse art is best described by which of these? 1. it has a social function of the reduction of surplus repression 2. it has self worth apart from any social consequences 3. its main value is due to its religious element 4. it is a means to achieving an inner harmony and peace of mind.

10. Wolff discusses three reasons why Plato's writings are works of art. Which of the following is one of these reasons? 1. they use language which is poetic 2. they contain realistic charters 3. they adopt the dialogue format 4. they make brilliant use of such devices as irony.

11. This individual is associated with the romantic movement in art. 1. Wilde 2. Tolstoy 3. Wordsworth 4. Marcuse.

12. What is the treatise of Aristotle that deals with the topic of art? 1. Republic 2. Intentions 3. What is Art? 4. Poetics.

13. One of the major elements of art for Tolstoy which is the source of its "infectiousness" is: 1. the religious language which is used 2. the sincerity of the artist 3. its appeals to the higher faculties in man like his reason 4. its effect on the soul in producing inner harmony.

14. Does the romantic view of art claim that art has an instrumental value? 1. yes 2. no.

15. Wolff uses this dialogue of Plato to illustrate the appearance-reality distinction. 1. Republic 2. Poetics 3. Gorgias 4. Intentions.

SELF TEST II

1. Explain the parable of the singers which Wolff presents at the beginning of the chapter.

2. Discuss the objections that Plato raises to art. Do you think they are reasonable objections?

3. Formulate in your own words what you think is Marcuse's theory of art.

4. Does Aristotle present any real rebuttal to the objections that Plato brings up against art? Explain your answer.

5. What are the main features of the romantic view of art and how do they differ from neoclassicism?

6. Explain the distinction between instrumental and intrinsic value and what this has to do with theories of art.

7. Philosophy of art is often understood as the study of beauty. Wolff, though, takes a different approach in this chapter. What would you say is the fundamental question of art from his prespective?

8. Briefly outline Tolstoy's view of art.

9. Classify the following thinkers as taking (1) the intrinsic view of art or (2) the instrumental view or (3) niether of these views.
   a. Plato
   b. Aristotle
   c. Wilde
   d. Wordsworth
   e. Tolstoy
   f. Marcuse

10. What are some features of Plato's dialogues that make them works of art according to Wolff?

Chapter Six

Philosophy of Religion

Study Suggestions

This chapter contains a few concepts that you need to be careful with. The first one is Kierkegaard's concept of "faith." You may, certainly, have your own concept of what faith is, but do make sure you understand his use of the expression, and specifically, what he means by "faith in God." A second idea that is central to Kierkegaard's position is the "leap of faith," so be sure you understand it also. In section II on the arguments for God's existence, Anselm's ontological argument is, probably, the most difficult one to understand. I would suggest that you read the Anselm selection, then Wolff's explanation which follows it, and then reread the Anselm passage. Also, refer to the section in the Study Guide that deals with the argument. Wolff has also warned you of the difficulty of the Kant selection, and before you read it, be sure to know the meanings of the terms "analytic" and "synthetic."

Chapter Overview

This chapter is a general survey of some of the philosophical issues and problems associated with Western religious thought. Three main issues are examined: the problem of faith, the proof of God, and the value of religion. Kierkegaard's religious philosophy is presented as an example of how one thinker has addressed the issue of faith. This is followed by a discussion of three arguments for God's existence: the argument from design, the cosmological argument, and the ontological argument.

Freud's views of the nature of religion complete the chapter.

Chapter Analysis

Section I

The first several paragraphs provide some important biographical information about Kierkegaard that has a bearing on his religious philosophy, so dont gloss over them too quickly.

Professor Wolff then lists three interrelated factors which dominated Kierkegaard's life and form the basis for understanding his view of religion. They are:
1.   his inner emotional life.
2.   his struggle with faith.
3.   his reaction to Hegel's philosophy.
The rest of this section is structured on an examination of these three elements.

Kierkegaard's inner life and thought focused on the notion of "existential dread" which must not be understood as merely a fear associated with our own death. It has to do with what death brings which is the end of our very being, a final, total termination of our existence. It seems to negate any meaning that life might have had. I think that it is important, here, that you do not confuse the kind of fear of death that Kierkegaard is talking about with a fear of dying. The two are not the same. The latter fear -that of dying- is concerned with the actual dying process and things like whether it involves extreme pain and so forth.

For Kierkegaard, this dread of death is juxtaposed with the element of religious hope; religious hope in the sense of a continued life after death or eternal life. Pay close attention to Wolff's description of what "faith" or "faith in God" means for Kierkegaard and how it is related to eternal life. The last sentence of the seventh paragraph is a good summary of it.

Wolff next examines what he calls the "central religious problem" for Kierkegaard, which is the problem of faith. The problem has to do with accepting God's promise of life eternal without any reservation or doubt. God's offer is not conditioned on anything that man could do like good works to atone for his sins since that has already been accomplished by the sacrifice of Christ. What is required is unqualified faith.

In addressing the problem of faith there were "three enemies" that Kierkegaard had to deal with according to Wolff. They are:
1. The established Christianity of his time.
2. The middle-class of his society.
3. The accepted philosophical system of his time -Hegelianism.

They are enemies because they are a hindrance to the proper understanding and practice of religion, at least as Kierkegaard views religion. Even though the three are individually examined there is an interrelationship between them, and Wolff discussed it before he presents Kierkegaard's attack.

The two major concepts of Kierkegaard's view of religion which Wolff discussed in some detail are:
1. The subjectivity of truth.
2. The leap of faith.

This notion of the subjectivity of truth is the reversal of the concept of truth that was current in the philosophy and science of Kierkegaard's time. Wolff devotes several paragraphs to discussing the older idea of truth which is usually called the correspondence theory of truth. This theory presents truth as a relationship between a statement and some state of affairs. The idea is this: the statement is true if it corresponds with the state of affairs to which it refers; if it does not correspond to it, then it is false. Truth is objective since it depends only on the relation of the statement to the world, and furthermore, the relationship is open to public inspection. Note that it would be irrelevant to take into account the individual who puts forth the statement; the person who makes the statement has nothing to do with its truth or falsity. It is this feature of the older theory to which Kierkegaard objects. For him, truth _must_ involve the individual. Here is Wolff's statement of Kierkegaard's position on truth: truth "consists in the proper relationship between the belief and the subject... How he or she holds it is the criterion of its truth." Here is another case where you may be inclined to disagree with a thinker's view (which is fine), but make sure you do not confuse not accepting his view with not understanding it. As I have said before, seek understanding first, and then decide whether you accept or reject the view.

The other fundamental concept in Kierkegaard's religious philosophy is the leap of faith. Remember that the term faith means an unquestioned belief in God's promise of eternal life. The "leap of faith" refers to the fact that there can be no proof or argument to support or justify this belief about God. For Kierkegaard, the leap of faith is irrational, but absolutely necessary. This idea is more fully explained by Wolff in the paragraph on Kierkegaard's <u>Philosophical Fragments</u>, so you might want to reread it.

Section II

You may already be familiar with some of the information in this section which deals with arguments for God's existence. Here, Wolff examines the following proofs:
1. The argument from design -Paley's version.
2. The cosmological argument - Aquinas' versions.
3. The ontological argument - Anselm's version.

The first argument -the argument from design- is also referred to in philosophical literature as the teleological argument. The argument is fairly easy to understand if you note these two features: its structure and the basic concept it employs. Beginning with the later, the argument is based on the idea of either order or purpose; that is, the term design can be understood in either of these ways. Let's consider the concept of order and the argument would be this: A careful observation of the universe will reveal innumerable instances of order. A macroscopic view (the large view) would reveal such order as the day-night sequence or the seasonal changes all of which are based on the orderly movement of the earth. There is all of the planetary and galactic motion which reflects order. At the microscopic level, the behavior of the atoms and molecules is orderly. The argument maintains that the degree and complexity of all the order cannot be due to chance occurrence or accident and that there must be an author to the order. That author is God. This argument is structured on the method of analogical reasoning. The analogy is this: the universe is like an orderly machine or clock and as a machine or clock has a machine maker or clock maker to explain its existence, so must the universe have an author.

The two objections that Wolff brings up are these:
1. Even if the argument is valid it does not prove anything more than that the universe was ordered by something. The argument is silent on what, if any, relationship would exist between God and man.
2. The conclusion, that God exists, does not follow from the premises that state that order exists. The so called order may only be an appearance, and secondly, if it does exist, there is no compelling reason why it would have to have some author.

The cosmological argument is considered next. Here, Wolff gives, in outline form, a summary of three of Aquinas' five arguments. This is followed by his own example to illustrate the nature of this form of argument. The basis of the cosmological argument is the observation of some particular feature of the universe such as motion or even the mere existence of any individual. The argument maintains that in each case there is a <u>sequence</u> of causes that have brought about the event -say, the motion or the individual. The question is raised as to whether the sequence of causes goes back in time forever or whether there is a stopping point -a first cause. The argument claims that an infinite regress of causes is impossible, and therefore, there must be a First Cause which is God. It is important to note that God is not merely the first event in a long causal series of events, but rather the First Cause of <u>all</u> causal sequences of events.

The Hume selection is used to illustrate the kinds of objections that have been raised against the argument. His objection to the above version is that if all the individual events can be explained on the basis of individual causes, then there is no need to look for some cause for the <u>whole</u> sequence of events. The whole sequences of events is the collection of the individual parts and if they have been explained, then so has the whole been explained.

The last and, perhaps, the most difficult argument is Anselm's ontological proof. As Wolff recommends, you should read the Anselm passage carefully in order to grasp his argument. The elements of this form of the argument are these:
1. It begins with the premise that all men have in their minds a concept of God.
2. Men conceive of God as a being than which nothing greater can be conceived.

It is this second element, which is Anselm's definition of God, that leads to the tautology to which Wolff refers. The expression "being than which nothing greater can be conceived" contains the idea of existence. There are several ways to analyze Anselm's argument, but to follow Wolff's approach, consider the argument in this way. Anselm is really saying that our concept of God is that God is perfect. Could God be perfect and exist only in our mind as merely a mental concept or idea? Anselm would say no, because if God existed only as a concept or idea, God would not be perfect. God would not be perfect because He would lack something, namely, an objective existence outside of one's mind. Thus, if God is perfect, then God must objectively exist. The ontological argument in its most condensed version is this: God's perfection implies His existence.

The Kant reading will give you an example of the kind of criticism that has been directed against the ontological argument. His critique is based on what is called the analytic-synthetic distinction. This is a pair of terms which are used to classify statements or propositions on the basis of the relationship of their subjects to their predicates. An analytic statement is one in which the subject term contains the predicate term. Synthetic statements have subjects which do not contain the predicate. Study Wolff's examples of both kinds of statements so that you have a good grasp of this distinction, since this is the basis of Kant's criticism. Two important characteristics of the distinction that should be pointed out are these:
1. The terms analytic and synthetic are mutually exclusive; that is, if a statement is classified as analytic, it cannot be also classified as synthetic.
2. The terms are jointly exhaustive; that is, there are no statements that cannot be classified as either analytic or synthetic.

The thrust of Kant's objection is this: If the statement "God exists" is analytic then the subject term "God" already contains the predicate term "exists," and consequently, this statement is a tautology and nothing has been proven. If the statement "God exists" is synthetic, then Kant's objection is that the term "existence" is not a predicate in the logical sense of the term. To state that God exists is not to predicate any attribute of God. So again, nothing has been proven.

Section III

If you have strong religious beliefs you may find this last section of the chapter either puzzling or offensive. It is wise to remember though, that not all people share the same outlook on religion, and one of the results of the study of philosophy should be the production of an open mind.

The substance of Freud's attack on religion, which begins in the third paragraph, can be summarized as this: religious ideas are illusions which are derived from our wishes. In the Freud reading, there is the explanation that individuals turn to religious beliefs as a way of resolving certain conflicts. It is in this sense that

religion is an opiate. It makes possible the acceptance of
much in the world that cannot be immediately changed. Freud
suggests that "an illusion is not the same an error," and
not all errors are to be classified as illusions either.
Therefore, he is forced to admit that illusions "need not
necessarily be false." However, although a few illusions
may turn out true, he has serious doubts about religious
beliefs having the same outcome.

Chapter Six Outline

Section One: Kierkegaard's Encounter With Faith

    I.   Kierkegaard's biography.

    II.   Kierkegaard and the dread of death.
        A.   The element of religious hope.
        B.   The element of faith.
        C.   The meaning of God's promise.

    III. The problem of faith.

    IV.   The enemies of religious faith.
        A.   Established Christianity.
        B.   Middle-class society.
        C.   Hegelian philosophy.
        D.   The relationship of these enemies.

    V.   Kierkegaard's position.
        A.   The subjectivity of truth.
            1.   The denial of objectivity.
            2.   The relation between belief and
                   subject.
        B.   The leap of faith.
            1.   The impossibility of proof.
            2.   The futility of reason.

    VI.   The argument in the <u>Philosophical Fragments</u>.
        A.   Secular knowledge.
            1.   The role of the teacher.
            2.   The role of reason.
        B.   Religious truth.
            1.   The nature of salvation.
            2.   The leap of faith.

    VII. Kierkegaard Reading.

Section Two: Can We Prove That God Exists?

    I.   Background material on proofs.

    II.   Paley's argument from design.
        A.   The analogical structure of the argument.
        B.   Two forms of the analogy.
        C.   Paley reading.

    III. Two criticisms of the argument.

        A.   Wolff's criticism.
        B.   Hume's criticism.

   IV.   The cosmological argument.
        A.   Two sources of belief about God.
              1.   Revelation.
              2.   Reason.
        B.   Aquinas' proofs.
        C.   Aquinas reading.

   V.   The ontological argument.
        A.   Anselm reading.
        B.   The structure of the argument.
              1.   The a priori element.
              2.   Tautologies.
              3.   Existence.
        C.   Kant's refutation.
              1.   The meaning of analytic.
              2.   The meaning of synthetic.

Section Three: Freud's Critique of Religion

   I.   The decline of religion in Western society.

   II.   Freud's view of reason.

   III. Freud's view of religion.
        A.   Religion as illusion.
        B.   Freud reading.

KEY TERMS

*Existentialism   A philosophical view that focuses on the question of human existence, its nature, meaning, and purpose. Kierkegaard is generally considered as the founder of the view.

Leap of Faith   An expression used by Kierkegaard to refer to the unquestioned acceptance of God's promise of salvation.

Analogy   A form of reasoning in which there is a comparison of the characteristics of two things that are similar in some way. The idea is that if the first thing has the characteristic, then the second thing, which is **like** (this is the key word in identifying analogical reasoning) it, must also have the characteristic.

Argument   A process of reasoning in which premises are offered in support of a conclusion. The idea is that the conclusion follows logically from the premises, if the argument is valid.

Revelation   A theological term that refers to the process of God giving to man certain information or knowledge.

Tautology   A statement which is true due to the meanings of its words.

Analytic   A classification term for statements in which the subject term contains the predicate term.

Synthetic   A classification term for statements in which the subject term does not contain the predicate.

A priori   A Latin term used in philosophy to refer to knowledge that is prior to or not based on experience. The ontological argument is classified as a priori since it is based on reason rather than on observation.

A posteriori	A Latin term used in philosophy to refer to knowledge which comes after experience or is based on experience. The cosmological and teleological arguments are classified as a posteriori since they are based on observation or experience.
Illusion	A Freudian term that refers to beliefs in which the prominent factor is a wish-fulfillment.

Check List of Important Items

TERMS

Faith	Philosophy of Religion	Hegelianism
Analogy	Subjective truth	Belief in God
Bourgeois	Existential dread	Leap of Faith
Revelation	Objective truth	A priori
Tautology	Argument from design	A posteriori
Analytic	Cosmological proof	Synthetic
Illusion	Ontological proof	Existentialism

THINKERS

Soren Kierkegaard	Georg Hegel
William Paley	David Hume
Immanuel Kant	Thomas Aquinas
Sigmund Freud	

WRITINGS

Concluding Unscientific Postscript to the Philosophical Fragments

Natural Theology

Dialogues Concerning Natural Religion

Summa Theologica

Proslogion

Critique of Pure Reason

The Future of an Illusion

SELF TEST I

1. The expression "belief in God" has which of the following meanings for Kierkegaard? 1. it means believing that God exists 2. it means believing that God loves man 3. it means believing that God will keep his promise of life eternal 4. it means believing that God is omnipotent, omniscient, and benevolent.

2. He is associated with the argument from design. 1. Paley 2. Anselm 3. Aquinas 4. Kierkegaard.

3. According to Freud, religion is best described by which of these? 1. man should turn to religion in order to live a meaningful life 2. religion is a fraud 3. only religion offers salvation to man 4. religion is essential for the survival of society.

4. This thinker put forth several versions of the cosmological argument.

   _____

5. One of the objections to the ontological argument is which of these? 1. that it is based on a false analogy 2. that existence is not a predicate 3. that the definition of God contains a contradiction 4. that God's perfection cannot be proven on the basis of observation.

6. For Kierkegaard, the basic problem of religion is proving that God exists.   True   False.

7. He describes religious beliefs as involving wish-fulfillment.

   _____

8. This argument for God's existence is classified as an a priori argument. 1. the argument from design 2. the cosmological argument 3. the teleological argument 4. the ontological argument.

9. Kant uses a certain distinction in his analysis of the ontological argument which concerns the classification of propositions into two groups. Which of the following is the distinction? 1. rational-irrational 2. analytic-synthetic 3. a priori-a posteriori 4. true-false.

10. In his religious philosophy, he takes the position that truth is subjective. 1. Kierkegaard 2. Kant 3. Anselm 4. Aquinas.

11. Kierkegaard used this expression to describe the manner in which man must believe in God when he has no proof or rational justification of God's existence.

    _____

12. One of the criticisms of the argument from design is: 1. it does not really prove the existence of a God like the God of Judaism or Christianity 2. existence is not a property of God that logically follows from His perfection 3. an infinite series of causal events can be explained on the basis of individual causes 4. the argument contains a tautology which is contradictory.

13. He is usually regarded as the founder of the philosophical movement called existentialism.

    _____.

14. The major critic of the ontological argument was: 1. Hume 2. Kant 3. Freud 4. Kierkegaard.

15. One of the major characteristics of this argument is its use of analogy. 1. the ontological argument 2. the cosmological argument 3. Kant's argument 4. the argument from design.

SELF TEST II

1. List and briefly describe the three enemies with which Kierkegaard struggled.

2. What is Freud's objection to religion and religious belief?

3. What is Kant's criticism of the ontological argument?

4. Explain the term "leap of faith" as Kierkegaard uses it in his religious philosophy.

5. Classify the arguments for God's existence on the basis of the terms a priori and a posteriori.

6. What is Hume's objection to the cosmological argument?

7.   What does Kierkegaard mean by the claim that truth is subjective?

8.   Give the two objections which Wolff presents to the argument from design.

9.   According to Kierkegaard what is the central problem of religion?

10. Present the argument from design in your own words.

Chapter Seven

Theory of Knowledge

Study Suggestions

The topics covered in this chapter tend to be more difficult to understand than those in the previous chapters. As you read the chapter, I would recommend that you use the rationalism-empiricism perspective as a reference for understanding the theories of Descartes, Leibniz, Locke, and Hume. That is, first, get a grasp of what is meant by rationalism, and then, see how the theories of Descartes and Leibniz reflect that view of knowledge. Do the same for empiricism. View Kant's theory as an attempt to overcome some of the negative consequences of rationalism and empiricism.

Chapter Overview

This chapter covers the branch of Philosophy called epistemology which deals with such issues as the extent, sources, and justification of knowledge claims. The two major schools of thought that are first examined are the following:
1. Rationalism -the view that knowledge must ultimately be grounded in reason.
2. Empiricism -the view that knowledge must ultimately be grounded in sense experience.

The first approach is illustrated by the theories of Descartes and Leibniz, and the second by the theories of Locke and Hume.

The concluding section of the chapter outlines Kant's theory which is not classified as a version of either rationalism or empiricism, but rather as a synthesis of both.

Chapter Analysis

Section I

After a brief synopsis of the various kinds of questions dealt with in the previous chapters, Wolff, in the second and third paragraphs through some hypothetical situations, raises some fundamental questions of epistemology. The next few paragraphs discuss the importance and difficulty of understanding the problems and effects of modern epistemology.

The rest of this section contains an exposition of Descartes' theory of knowledge. Wolff begins with a discussion of Descartes' "method" which he divides into two parts to simplify its explanation. There is a method of inquiry and a method of doubt, both of which rely on Descartes' "four rules" that are contained is the first reading. Wolff explains the method of inquiry to be a process used to find something out and not a process of proof. This is the point of the Euclidian geometry illustration.

The method of doubt is a process that is used to determine which statements have the characteristic of **certainty,** and it is only those statements that can express knowledge claims. I think the easiest way to understand Wolff's discussion of Descartes' method of doubt is to think in terms of the difference between Knowledge and belief or opinion. The difference can be succinctly stated in this way: knowledge implies certainty; whereas, beliefs imply some degree of doubt. Thus, any statement about which there is any kind of doubt cannot be a statement that expresses knowledge. This kind of statement might express belief or opinion. So, the method amounts to trying to raise some kind -any kind- of doubt about a given statement. If there is no way to bring doubt to bear on a given statement, then it passes the test and can be accepted as expressing knowledge.

The combination of the method of inquiry and the method of doubt is what Wolff calls the **epistemological turn.** Traditionally, philosophers have given priority to questions about what is real (metaphysical) over questions

concerning what can be known (epistemological). The
reversal of this order of priority is the **epistemological
turn**. This reference to metaphysics and epistemology
brings up an important point worth noting here. There is
an intimate relation between these areas in that all
theories of knowledge presuppose some theory of what is
real. For example, Descartes' metaphysical view is that of
dualism -the view that reality consists of both material
and non-material entities. His rationalism is a reflection
of this view, and indeed, Descartes is lead to this view of
reality through an examination of questions of knowledge.
So, for him, epistemology is the primary area.

The first section concludes with the rather lengthy
selection from Descartes **Meditations** which illustrates his
method of doubt.

Section II

Through the application of the method of doubt, Descartes
claimed to be able to doubt of everything except the
knowledge claim expressed by the statement, "I exist." In
this section, Wolff examines the well known Cogito Argument
of Descartes. Read carefully what he says here to see what
it is that Descartes proves.

There are two consequences that follow from Descartes'
argument:
  1.   It leads to the philosophical position of
        solipsism -the view that only the individual
        exists; everything else is only an idea in his
        mind.
  2.   It shifts the focus from the object of knowledge
        to the subject of knowledge -the "knower."

Next, two problems that are raised by arguments in the
First Meditation are discussed along with Descartes'
solutions. The problems are these:
  1.   What is the criterion of certainty for knowledge
        claims?
  2.   What are the sources of knowledge?
Both problems arise from Descartes' classification of
knowledge claims into two groups: knowledge claims based on
sense experience and knowledge claims based on general
principles. His solution to the problem of criteria is to
state that whatever is perceived with clearness and
distinction is to be accepted as true. God becomes an
essential element in Descartes theory, and although the
selected reading does not contain Descartes proof of God,
Wolff explains what role God plays in his system.

Descartes's answer to the second question is that reason must be the ultimate basis of knowledge. The last reading in this section illustrates his view of the role of reason.

The first three paragraphs following the last Descartes reading contain a good discussion of the differences between the positions of rationalism and empiricism.

Section III

The views of Leibniz, the second representative of rationalism, are outlined in this section. Wolff begins by offering a criticism of Descartes' criteria of truth, the doctrine of clearness and distinctness. The objection is that this test, which is psychological in nature, is highly subjective.

For Leibniz, there are two categories of truth:
1. Truths of reason -those claims that can be known on the basis of the laws of logic.
2. Truths of fact -those claims that cannot be known of the basis of the laws of logic.

The truths of reason are known on the basis of the law of contradiction which Wolff explains in the second and third paragraphs of this section. The law amounts to this claim: a statement and its negation cannot both be true at the same time. According to Wolff, there is also a second law of logic -the law of the excluded middle- that is used to know truths of reason.

Notice that these truths of reason are merely instances of these laws of logic and, as such, are not very informative. To know the truth of a claim like "the door is open or the door is not open" does not really tell one much about the door.

Empirical knowledge is what Leibniz calls truths of fact and is based on the principle of sufficient reason. For any factual statement to be certified as true, there must be a sufficient reason "why it should be thus and not otherwise." To know the truth of any given factual claim requires one to have knowledge of an infinite sequence of prior causes. This, in turn, becomes the basis for establishing the existence of God. By the way, since God knows the sufficient reason for all truths of fact, they are, for Him, necessary truths. So this distinction between truths of reason and truths of fact does not hold for God.

Section IV

This section is devoted to a consideration of empiricism, the contrasting theory of knowledge to rationalism. Here the claim is that knowledge is ultimately based on sense experience.

Locke's version of empiricism is taken up first. According to Locke's theory, ideas that are used in knowledge claims must come from experience. (See the first reading for Locke's expression of this.) Any idea that is not derived from sense experience cannot serve as part of a knowledge claim. After commenting on some of the consequences of this view, Wolff turns to an exposition of Hume's development of Locke's theory.

Wolff derives the following three elements from the Hume reading:
1. Hume's adoption of Locke's blank paper theory.
2. The development of the "copy theory."
3. The development of the "atomic theory" of the operation of the mind.

You will have to study the passage carefully to discover the first element. When Hume states that all simple ideas must have a simple impression, he is claiming essentially the same thing as did Locke -that the content of the mind is furnished by experience.

The "copy theory" that Wolff discusses is a reference to Hume's claim that all simple ideas correspond to what he calls impressions. The simple ideas that are produced by simple impressions are, in a sense, copies of these sense impressions. However, not all complex ideas are copies of things that have been observed. The mind can fashion some complex ideas out of a combination of simple ideas.

Wolff uses the term "atomic theory" to describe Hume's view that the basic constitutes of the mind are simple ideas which "admit of no distinction nor separation." In other words, the simple ideas of Hume are like atoms in that they are the smallest units with which the mind operates. Complex ideas are like molecules in that they are composed of smaller units, in this case, simple ideas.

According to Wolff, there are two principles that follow from the copy and atomic theories that Hume uses in arguments, and these result in the elimination of such things as natural science, metaphysics, and commonsense beliefs. Specifically, Hume's arguments are directed against the concept of events having causes. His first argument in the passage comes down to this: since the ideas of cause and effect are separate and distinct, it is possible to think of objects as existing or not existing without bringing in the idea of a cause; since this mental separation is possible, so is the actual separation possible. For Hume, this argument was a refutation of the principle "that whatever begins to exist, must have a cause of existence." There are other arguments in the passage, but this should give you a good idea of how Hume has applied some of the principles of his empiricism. Moreover, it is this kind of objection that strikes a serious blow to areas like science, metaphysics and religion, many of whose propositions are based on the principle of cause and effect.

Having completed this section on Hume, you may be wondering what it is that one can have certainty about. Hume's answer is, "Very little!" For Hume, one can have knowledge of the existence of the simple and complex ideas that are in one's mind. One cannot know if these ideas really match up with or are caused by anything that may exist outside the mind. It is for this reason, that many philosophers describe Hume's view as "radical empiricism." There is such a limitation to knowledge that Hume is only a few steps removed from skepticism -the view that knowledge or certain kinds of knowledge is impossible to acquire. Also, I think that you can see that Hume's position is heading in the direction of solipsism.

Section V

In this last section, Wolff surveys Kant's attempt to achieve a synthesis of rationalism and empiricism that would avoid some of the negative consequences of both.

The first three paragraphs review some of the features of Descartes system that Kant would use as the basis of a new approach to epistemology. Where previous thinkers erred was in their ignoring the consciousness of the mind. To be sure, Descartes and others were aware of this property, but they did not appreciate its significance.

You will probably find the next several paragraphs, which contain Wolff's analysis of Kant theory, to be difficult to follow. Kant's <u>Critique of Pure Reason</u> is, itself, forbiddingly difficult to read and comprehend, and so it is a formidable task to try to outline his views in a few pages. In what follows, I will give you a summary of the major points of Wolff's presentation of Kant, along with some supplemental information..

For Kant the most fundamental fact of consciousness is its unity which could only be explained on the basis of the existence of innate rules or categories. The categories represent ways in which the mind is structured and through which all experiences of the world are molded into knowledge. Space (not to be confused with a void or a container for matter) is an example of one of the categories. For Kant, space is a structure of our mind that is responsible for our experiencing objects as having three dimensions. In other words, we **bring** to our experience of an object a certain way of having that experience. We have no choice but to experience the object as having three dimensions; the dimensions are due to us, not the object. Notice, for Kant, knowledge has two components; one due to our mind and one due to our senses. But both of these components are unified in a single consciousness. The senses provide the input, while our reason provides the structure or form for what is known.

What Kant is attempting to do is to explain how we know, not what we know. Another point to note about Kant's view is how he avoids the subjectivity that was present in Descartes system. For Kant, the categories allow for objective judgments about reality because all persons have minds that are structured in the same manner; that is, all persons have the same categories. The skepticism of Hume is avoided because the individual can be absolutely certain of how things will be experienced. However, there is a price for this accomplishment; one cannot know how things really are, only how they appear.

Chapter Seven Outline

Section One: Descartes' Method of Doubt

  I.   Examples of questions about knowledge.

  II. Descartes' biography.

  III. Four rules.

  IV. The method of Descartes.
       A.   The method of inquiry.
       B.   The method of doubt.
            1.   The application of the first rule.
            2.   The certainty of one's existence.
       C.   The "epistemological turn."

  V.   Selections from Descartes' "Meditations."

Section Two: Rationalism and Empiricism: Two Responses to
                Cartesian Doubt

  I.   Descartes' Cogito Argument.
       A.   Two consequences.
            1.   Solipsism.
            2.   The focus on mind.

  II. Two problems of knowledge.
       A.   The problem of certainty.
       B.   The problem of the sources of knowledge.

  III. Descartes' solution.
       A.   The criteria of clearness and distinctness.
       B.   Reason as the foundation of knowledge.

  IV. Rationalism versus Empiricism.

Section Three: Leibniz and Rationalism

  I.   Leibniz's logical criteria of truth.
       A.   The law of contradiction.
       B.   The law of the excluded middle.

  II. Two kinds of truth.
       A.   Truths of reason.
            1.   The application of the laws.
            2.   The certainty of truths of reason.
       B.   Truths of fact.

            1.   The principle of sufficient reason.
            2.   The role of God.

    III. The "Monadology" Reading.

Section Four: Hume and Empiricism

    I.   Locke's view.
          A.   The role of experience.
          B.   The role of the mind.
                1.   The nature of ideas.
                2.   The source of ideas.

    II.   Hume's empiricism.
          A.   The role of perceptions.
          B.   Major elements of his view.
                1.   The blank paper theory.
                2.   The copy theory.
                3.   The "atomic theory."
          C.   Hume's argument: the application of his
                empiricism.
          D.   The consequences: the elimination of
                science, metaphysics, and common knowledge.

Section Five: Kant's Resolution of the
                Rationalism-Empiricism Debate

    I.   Kant's reaction to Hume's skepticism.

    II.   Kant's return to the Cartesian approach.
          A.   The role of consciousness.
          B.   The structure of consciousness.
                1.   Its unity.
                2.   The operation of rules or categories.
                3.   The relation of the categories to the
                      external world.

    III. The consequences of Kant's solution.

KEY TERMS

Epistemology
: The branch of philosophy that studies the nature of knowledge, its extent, sources, and justification.

Method of Doubt
: A process used by Descartes to discover which propositions could be known with certainty.

Method of inquiry
: A process used by Descartes to find things out.

Epistemological turn
: A term used by Wolff to indicate the reversal of the order of priority of metaphysics and epistemology where the latter takes precedence over the former.

Cogito Argument
: The argument formulated by Descartes that implied the certainty of his existence. The term "cogito" is derived from the Latin phrase "Cogito, ergo sum," which means "I think, therefore I am."

*Solipsism
: An extreme philosophical view that claims that only my mind exists and everything else is only an idea in my mind.

Rationalism
: The theory of knowledge that claims that all knowldege is ultimately gorunded in reason. For the rationalist, the primary source of knowledge is reason.

Empiricism
: The theory of knowledge that claims that all knowledge is ultimately grounded in sense experience. For the empiricist, sense experience is the primary source of knowledge.

*Law of contradiction
: A law of logic that states that a proposition and its negation cannot both be true at the same time.

90

*The excluded middle	A law of logic that states that either a proposition is true or its negation is true.
Truths of reason	An expression used by Leibniz to refer to the class of true claims based on the laws of logic.
Truths of fact	An expression used by Leibniz to refer to the class of truths based on the principle of sufficient reason.
Impressions	A term used by Hume to denote the kind of perception which enters the mind "with most force and violence." The term impression refers to the content derived directly from sense experience.
Categories	A term used by Kant to denote the concepts with which the mind is structured. Wolff describes categories as rules "for holding thoughts together in the mind."
Unity of consciousness	A term used by Kant to refer to the unity of all thoughts, feelings,beliefs, etc. in a single consciousness.

Check List of Important Items

TERMS

Epistemology
Copy theory
Categories
Method of inquiry
Epistemological turn
Argument
Cogito, ergo sum
Law of contradiction
Law of excluded middle
Principle of sufficient reason

Rationalism
Method of doubt
Empiricism
Solipsism
Impressions
Valid
Truth of reason
Invalid
Truths of fact

THINKERS

Rene Descartes   David Hume
John Locke   George Berkeley
Gottfried Leibniz   Immanuel Kant

WRITINGS

Meditations on First Philosophy

Discourse on Method

Treatise of Human Nature

Essay Concerning Human Understanding

The Monadology

Critique of Pure Reason

SELF TEST I

1. Epistemology deals with which of the following kinds
    of questions? 1. What is the nature of reality? 2.
    What is the good life? 3. What are the sources of
    knowledge? 4. Should society be based on liberty or
    equality for all?

2. Wolff discusses two features of Descartes' method.
    What does he call the process that is used to find
    things out?

    _____

3. This view claims that the source of all knowledge is
    reason. 1. solipsism 2. empiricism 3. skepticism
    4. rationalism.

4. What does Wolff call the process of reversing the
    order of priority of metaphysics and epistemology?

    _____

5. Which of the following thinkers are classified as
    empiricists? 1. Locke 2. Kant 3. Leibniz 4.
    Descartes.

6. The Cogito argument is best described by which of the
    following? 1. it is an argument that proves the
    existence of God 2. it is an argument that proves the
    the certainty of impressions 3. it is a proof of the
    existence of the person presenting the argument 4. it
    is the proof of truths of reason.

7. This law states that a proposition and its negation cannot both be true at the same time. 1. the law of the excluded middle 2. the principle of sufficient reason 3. the law of contradiction 4. the principle of identity.

8. The claim that the primary source of all knowledge is sense experience. 1. empiricism 2. rationalism 3. existentialism 4. phenomenalism.

9. According to Kant, the mind or consciousness has a unity which is due to certain rules which he called _____.

10. Which of the following thinkers would be classified as rationalists? 1. Descartes 2. Locke 3. Berekely 4. Hume.

11. For Leibniz, there are two kinds of truths. What is the name of the class of truths which are based on the laws of logic?
    _____

12. Which philosopher would you associate with the expression "I think, therefore I am?" 1. Leibniz 2. Locke 3. Kant 4. Descartes.

13. This philosopher uses God as the basis of the reliability of sense experience. 1. Descartes 2. Locke 3. Hume 4. Kant.

14. One of the problems of empiricism that was discussed was which of these? 1. it leads to skepticism 2. it is too subjective 3. one can have knowledge only if God exists 4. it relies to heavily on the use of reason.

15. The philosopher attempted to resolve the dispute between the rationalists and the empiricists.
    _____

SELF TEST II

1. Briefly explain the theory of knowledge called empiricism.

2. What role do laws of logic play in Leibniz's system and why is he classified as a rationalist?

3. Explain the two methods of Descartes that Wolff discussed.

4. What is meant by the "epistemological turn?" Why is it significant?

5. What are some of the problems with Hume's empiricism?

6. How does Kant's theory eliminate some of the problems of Hume's empiricism?

7. What role does God play in Leibniz's system?

8. If Descartes' proof of God is not valid, what would be the consequences for his theory of knowledge?

9. Explain Locke's "white Paper" theory.

10. What is the difference between impressions and ideas according to Hume?

Chapter Eight

Metaphysics and Philosophy of Mind

Study Suggestions

You should not find this chapter quite as difficult as the last one, but this is not to suggest that it is easy . As you read section II, take note of the three questions that Wolff poses because the rest of the section is structured on Leibniz's answers to these. Also, there are a few basic ideas you will need to deal with; the first is the concept of substance. Aristotle's definition of this is clearly explained and illustrated with examples, so read that section carefully. The second idea is Leibniz's concept of a monad. Study the Leibniz selection to see what his explanation is and pay close attention to Wolff's exposition that follows. Finally, when you get to section III, do not let the subtitle mislead you. There are four theorists discussed but only **three** body-mind theories.

Chapter Overview

This chapter is an introduction to the branch of philosophy that examines such issues as the nature of being, reality, and God. The chapter begins with an extensive list of the various kinds of metaphysical questions and continues with a discussion of Leibniz's theory of monads. The remainder of the chapter is devoted to an examination of the body-mind problem along with three proposed solutions.

Chapter Analysis

Section I

This section answers the question, "What is metaphysics?" in an indirect manner by listing the various kinds of questions that this branch of philosophy deals with. However, these questions should give you a good idea of what metaphysics is about. Further, there are no answers provided to the questions in this section, but later sections will deal with some of these issues.

Section II

The first three paragraphs give you some background material on Liebniz, and the fourth introduces one of the important concepts that is used throughout the rest of the chapter -the concept of substance.

The initial discussion concerns language and the use of subject and predicate terms. The upshot of the discussion is Aristotle's definition of substance as a kind of "ultimate" subject. For Aristotle, substance has to do with the essence of a thing; what it is that makes the thing what it is. This probably sounds like double-talk but what he means is that substance is "that which is not asserted of a subject but of which everything else is asserted." Attributes are the various properties which can be predicated of subjects. You may need to reread the fourth, fifth, and sixth paragraphs to be sure you grasp the meaning of **substance**.

As Wolff points out in a later paragraph, the notion of substance is fundamental to metaphysical theories that attempt to give an account of the universe.

Next, there is an examination of three answers to the question, "What kinds of substances make up the universe?" Below is a summary of the three:
    1.   The basic substance is atoms.
    2.   A basic substance is mind -a nonphysical entity.
    3.   God is the basic substance.
Wolff briefly discusses these three answers along with some representative thinkers. The point of the discussion is that there is genuine disagreement among thinkers about the basic nature of the universe.

The preceding discussion of substance and this last concern with different theories of the universe form a background against which Leibniz's theory is presented. But before Wolff considers the specifics of the theory, he presents three questions that it was designed to answer.

The first question is this: "What is the nature of the
basic substance dealt with by scientific laws?" Leibniz's
answer is that **monads** are the fundamental substance of
reality, and they have the following characteristics:
1. they are unextended, having no shape or size.
2. they are simple, having no parts.
3. each monad is independent from all other monads.
4. they are not created nor destroyed by natural
    processes; Leibniz says they are created by God.
5. each monad is different form other monads.
6. each monad contains, within itself, a principle
    of change.
7. they are conscious.
8. they are windowless.
Monads are somewhat like atoms in that they constitute all
of the commonsense objects of the world. These objects
-tables, chairs, trees, mountains, and the like- can be
destroyed but not the monads which make them up. Common
objects are collections of monads. Note this curious
feature of Leibniz's theory: monads have no dimensions,
but somehow an aggregate or collection of them -a physical
object- has shape, size, and dimension. It is as though
something new comes into being when monads group together.
Here, the whole is more than the sum of the parts.
Perhaps, this is not so strange. Consider some piece of
complicated machinery; certainly, it has characteristics,
as a whole machine, that its individual parts do not have.

The second question that Leibniz's theory answers concerns
the relationship that exists between the monads. His
answer is that there is none, at least, no external cause
and effect relation. Indeed, his answer could not be
otherwise, given the characteristcs he claims that monads
have. When monads are described as "windowless," Leibniz
means that they are not affected by anything that is
external to them; hence, they cannot causally interact with
one another. The problem is that they seem to interact.
For example, the collection of monads that constitute my
physical body seem to respond to the thoughts, feelings,
emotions, and beliefs that are in my mind, which is a
separate and independent monad from those that make up my
body. Also, physical objects seem to causally interact
with one another, and since they are collections of monads,
it would appear, therefore, that monads interact.

According to Wolff, this brings us to the third question of
God's relation to substance. For Leibniz, God exists as
the creator of the monads and of something called
pre-established harmony. The doctrine of pre-established
harmony not only explains God's relation to the monads, it

also provides a solution to the above stated problem. The idea of pre-established harmony is this: God has created the monads with an internal program of change that reflects all of the external things that go on outside the monad. All monads are pre-programed by God in this way. The orderly behavior of the universe is not due to cause and effect, rather to the internal principle of change within each monad.

If Leibniz was attempting to construct a theoretical foundation for the developing science of his day, he has ended up with a rather curious result. Physical laws which describe cause and effect reactions are really describing a pre-established harmony. Apparently, the only real case of cause and effect is God's causing the monads to exist and causing the pre-established harmony.

Section III

"What relationship exists between the body and the mind?" The significance of this question and some of the answers which have been proposed to it are the focus of this section. The significance of the question has to do with the fact that human beings are conscious, that they have self-awareness. Since the body is physical and can have only physical properties, what becomes of consciousness. Is it the property of something? What? The mind?

The three paragraphs after the first discuss some of the concerns of thinkers relating to the existence of mind and body. Descartes' theory of the relation of mind and body is briefly examined in the following paragraphs.

Descartes' metaphysical theory -called dualism- states that there exists both material and nonmaterial entities, that both are real. Further, man is an instance of this dualism being a union of body and mind. The mind, whose main attribute is thought, exists independently from the body, whose main attribute is extension. The problem that arises is that of the relation between these two different things. This is the so-called "body-mind" problem. Descartes' solution to the problem is the theory of interactionism. Although this theory is not specifically explained in Wolff's text, I think it will be helpful to you in understanding Descartes' views. The theory of interactionism states that there is a cause and effect relation between mental events (some, not all) that take place in the mind and physical events (some, not all) that take place in the body; the reverse is also true. For example, a thought -the mental event- may cause some bodily behavior like running -the physical event. Of course, the thought could have also caused several other thoughts or mental events as well as the physical event of running. For Descartes, this theory of interactionism not only explained the relation of the mind to the body, it also supplied a kind justification for the existence of mental phenomenon. If consciousness has no consequences in the physical realm, then why postulate its existence? Why bother with an examination of its nature?   There are problems with the theory which cannot be covered here, but this should give you a good idea of what Descartes proposed as a solution to the body-mind problem.

After discussing Descartes, Wolff presents three metaphysical views that have dominated Western thinking about the body-mind issue. These are materialism, idealism, and dualism. Dualism has already been covered above, and since the rest of this section deals with materialism ,I will only summarize the view of idealism here.

So that you do not misunderstand these views, let me say, first, that materialism, idealism, and dualism are not merely views about the body-mind problem. They are metaphysical theories about the nature of reality. Each theory has some implications for the body-mind issue, so, in that sense, they can be considered as containing solutions.

Idealism is the view that only nonmaterial things are real. Plato and Berkeley are two thinkers who took this position. Now, idealism is a solution to the body-mind problem only in a negative sense. Since physical bodies are not real there is no relationship to explain; no problem exists!

The remainder of this section is devoted to an examination of materialism, the view that only physical matter is real, and the main representative of this position is Thomas Hobbes. Materialism is a solution to body mind problem, also, in a negative sense. For the materialist, the mind does not exist as a nonmaterial thing. Furthermore, "mental" processes like thinking, wishing, willing, and doubting must be interpreted as physical processes. For example, thinking could be described as a neural-chemical process that takes place in the brain. As you read the Hobbes selection, notice his analysis of the various processes like sense experience and imagination. In every case, these are the result of motions that take place on the basis of cause and effect. His view is sometimes called mechanistic materialism. Man is like a machine whose operation is wholly dependant on causes. Thus, "mental" processes are really physical or mechanical processes and there is no need to postulate the existence of something called the mind.

The second part of the last sentence may seem to be contradicted by what Wolff says in the first paragraph following the Hobbes reading. Wolff, in describing Hobbes' position, says minds are bodies, and "there is no reason why the two should not interact." His reference to "two" things interacting may mislead you. If the mind **is** the body, then there is only one thing that exists or is real, not two.

The problem of materialism is whether this doctrine does justice to our experience of reality, which includes such things as the fact of our awareness or consciousness. Does materialism adequately account for "mental" phenomenon. This debate continues and is the underlying theme of the next two readings.

As is clear from the reading, Smart is an avowed materialist who denies the existence of nonphysical things, as well as nonphysical laws. He does not believe that the (biological) evolutionary process could ever result in the production of nonphysical properties of animals.

The Malcolm reading must be read carefully, in order to grasp his objection. Specifically, he arguing against the **identity** of mental and physical processes. Materialists, like Smart, attempt to account for consciousness by explaining it as a physical process. One of Malcolm's arguments amounts to this: that mental processes cannot be the same as physical processes, because physical processes have properties like spatial location, which mental processes cannot have. Thus, the two cannot be identical.

Chapter Eight Outline

Section One: What is Metaphysics?

    I.   Metaphysical questions.
-   A.   Questions about what exists.
-   B.   Questions about concepts.
-   C.   Questions about the processes of reality.
-   D.   Questions about the existence of God.

Section Two: Leibniz's Theory of Monads

    I.   Leibniz biography.

    II.   The concept of substance.
-   A.   Aristotle's concept.
-   B.   The concept of attributes.
-   C.   Understanding the universe.

    III.   Three views of substance.
-   A.   Substance as material -atoms.
-   B.   Substance as mental - mind.
-   C.   Substance as God.

    IV.   Three fundamental questions.
-   A.   The basic substances of science.
-   B.   The relationships between basic substances.
-   C.   God's relationship to substance.

    V.   The theory of monads.
-   A.   Monads as nonmaterial centers of energy.
-   B.   Monads as windowless.
-   C.   The pre-estaablished harmony of monads.

Section Three: The relation of the Mind to the Body: Four Theorists

    I.   The universe and purposive order.
-   A.   Traditional views.
-   B.   Descartes' view.

    II.   The body-mind problem.
-   A.   Traditional views.
-   B.   Descartes' view.

    III.   Solutions to the problem.
-   A.   Materialism.
-   B.   Idealism.
-   C.   Dualism.

IV.   The theory of Hobbes.
        A.   His version of materialism.
        B.   The problem of materialism.

V.   The theory of Smart.

VI.   The criticism of Malcolm.

KEY TERMS

Metaphysics The branch of philosophy that studies such things as the nature of reality, the nature of being, and the nature of God.

Substance In metaphysics, that which can have properties predicated of it, but cannot, itself, be a predicate for any object.

Attribute A property or characteristic that is predicated of some subject.

Monads A term used by Leibniz to refer to the basic substance of reality. Monads are nonextened, nonmaterial centers of energy or force.

*Pre-established harmony The term used by Leibniz to explain the relationships between monads. Each monad is pre-programmed, by God, with an inner principle of order that reflects the order of all that is external to the monad.

*The body-mind problem The problem of explaining what kind of relationship exists between the body and the mind or between mental events and physical events.

Materialism The metaphysical view that claims that only nonphysical entities are real or exist. It denies the reality or existence of nonmaterial things.

Idealism The metaphysical view that claims that only nonphysical entities are real or exist. It denies the reality or existence of material things.

Dualism The metaphysical view that claims that reality consists of both material and nonmaterial entities.

Descartes is the best known
representative of this view.

The identity theory A theory that explains mental
events as physical processes. The
idea is that mental phenomenon are
reducible to certain physical
processes that take place in the
brain.

Check List of Important Items

TERMS

Pre-established harmony   Substance
Metaphysics   Idealism
Body-mind problem   Materialism
Dualism   Attribute
Monads   Consciousness
Mental phenomenon   Virtual
Actual   Identity theory

THINKERS

Gottfried Leibniz
Aristotle   Rene Descartes
Thomas Hobbes   J.J.C. Smart
                Norman Malcolm

WRITINGS

The Monadology

Leviathan

"Materialism"

"Scientific Materialism and the Identity Theory"

SELF TEST I

1. According to Wolff, metaphysics deals with that which
transcends sense experience. 1. True 2. False.

2. This view denies the reality of nonphysical things.
1. idealism 2. materialism 3. dualism 4. Malcolm's
theory.

3. For Aristotle, which of the following is the definition of substance? 1. anything that has attributes 2. anything that has characteristics 3. anything that can be the subject of predication but cannot itself be predicated of anything 4. anything that is material and has only physical properties like location in space.

4. The metaphysical position of Descartes is which of these? 1. dualism 2. idealism 3. materialism 4. the one-substance theory.

5. The issue of the relation of the body to the mind is called the _____.

6. Which of the following is the best description of a monad? 1. they are uncreated, physical entities like atoms 2. they are created by God as substances that causally interact with souls 3. they are nonphysical centers of consciousness 4. they are substances totally without attributes.

7. This term is used to explain the relationship that exists between the monads.
_____.

8. Which of these views represents the position of Malcom? 1. the body and the mind are identical 2. mental phenomenon and brain phenomenon are different 3. mental events are neural-chemical processes that take place in the brain 4. mental phenomenon are the basic substances of reality.

9. This individual is one of the main representatives of the doctrine of materialism. 1. Descartes 2. Malcolm 3. Leibniz 4. Hobbes.

10. According to Wolff, what relationship exists between the areas of science and metaphysics for Leibniz? 1. metaphysics provides the theoretical foundation for science 2. metaphysics provides a causal proof for scientific laws 3. metaphysics defines the fundamental concepts used in scientific laws 4. there is no relationship between the two for Leibniz.

11. The term metaphysics is the result of the classification of the writings of which of these thinkers? 1. Plato 2. Aristotle 3. Socrates 4. Leibniz.

12. Leibniz's theory of reality is best described by which of these? 1. Dualism 2. Materialism 3. the two-substance theory 4. Idealism.

13. The ancient cosmologists explained reality in terms of what basic substance?

   _____

14. This is the term that was fundamantal to Aristotle's philosophy of "first principles" or metaphysics. 1. God 2. attribute 3. appearance 4. essence.

15. He is a contemporary philosopher who defends the postion of materialism.

   _____

SELF TEST II

1. List some representative questions of metaphysics. Explain why they are examples of this.

2. In your own words, explain Leibniz's concept of a monad.

3. What is the body-mind problem?

4. Discuss Descartes' answer to the body mind-problem.

5. In answer to the question about what kinds of substances make up the universe, Wolff states that there are three major answers that thinkers have proposed. What are they?

6. Briefly state Hobbes' view of reality.

7. What is Malcolm's objection to Smart's position?

8. According to Wolff, what are the three questions that must be answered by any philosophical theory that attempts to provide a foundation for science?

9. Discuss a criticism of materialism.

10. Explain what Wolff means by the following terms: one-substance theory, two-substance theory.

ANSWER KEY

This section contains answers to all questions in Self Test I for each chapter. The answer is either the number of the correct choice or the correct term for filling in the blank.

Chapter 1

1. - 2
2. - 2
3. - 3
4. - Lucretius
5. - the nature of man
6. - 2
7. - 4
8. - epistemology
9. - 2
10. - false
11. - <u>Gorgias</u>
12. - 1
13. - Socrates
14. - true
15. - the dialectical method

Chapter 2

1. - 2
2. - Jeremy Bentham
3. - reason
4. - 4
5. - 4
6. - Erikson
7. - <u>Republic</u>
8. - 1
9. - 3
10. - Ruth Benedict
11. - 1
12. - 4
13. - 1
14. - 2
15. - 1

Chapter 3

1. - false
2. - 2
3. - true
4. - in quantity, in quality
5. - 2
6. - 1
7. - 4
8. - false
9. - 1
10. - false
11. - Jeremy Bentham
12. - 1
13. - 1
14. - human reason
15. - 2

Chapter 4

1. - 2
2. - Fascism
3. - Burke
4. - the means of production
5. - 2
6. - 3
7. - 2
8. - Anarchism
9. - 4
10. - 1
11. - 2
12. - 1
13. - Proletariat
14. - 1
14. - 2

Chapter 5

1.   - imagination
2.   - 4
3.   - 2
4.   - 4
5.   - 2
6.   - 2
7.   - 1
8.   - 2
9.   - 1
10. - 2
11. - 3
12. - 4
13. - 2
14. - 1
15. - 1

Chapter 6

1.   - 3
2.   - 1
3.   - 2
4.   - Aquinas
5.   - 2
6.   - false
7.   - Freud
8.   - 4
9.   - 2
10. - 1
11. - leap of faith
12. - 1
13. - Kierkegaard
14. - Kant
15. - 4

Chapter 7

1.   - 3
2.   - method of inquiry
3.   - 4
4.   - epistemological turn
5.   - 1
6.   - 3
7.   - 3
8.   - 1
9.   - categories
10. - 1
11. - truths of reason
12. - 4
13. - 1
14. - 1
15. - Kant

Chapter 8

1.   - 2
2.   - 2
3.   - 3
4.   - 1
5.   - body-mind problem
6.   - 3
7.   - pre-established harmony
8.   - 2
9.   - 4
10. - 1
11. - 2
12. - 4
13. - atoms
14. - 4
15. - Smart